100

Best Fresh
Soups

100

Best Fresh
Soups

The ultimate ingredients for delicious soups including 100 tasty recipes

This edition published in 2012
LOVE FOOD is an imprint of Parragon Books Ltd

Parragon
Queen Street House
4 Queen Street
Bath BA1 1HE, UK

www.parragon.com

ISBN: 978-1-4454-6199-1

Printed in Indonesia

Photography by Mike Cooper
Food styling by Carole Handslip and Sumi Glass
Introduction by Pamela Gwyther

Notes for the Reader
This book uses both metric and imperial measurements. Follow the same units of measurement throughout; do not mix metric and imperial. All spoon measurements are level: teaspoons are assumed to be 5 ml, and tablespoons are assumed to be 15 ml. Unless otherwise stated, milk is assumed to be full fat, eggs and individual vegetables are medium, and pepper is freshly ground black pepper.

The times given are an approximate guide only. Preparation times differ according to the techniques used by different people and the cooking times may also vary from those given. Optional ingredients, variations or serving suggestions have not been included in the calculations.

Recipes using raw or very lightly cooked eggs should be avoided by infants, the elderly, pregnant women, convalescents and anyone suffering from an illness. Pregnant and breastfeeding women are advised to avoid eating peanuts and peanut products. Sufferers from nut allergies should be aware that some of the ready-made ingredients used in the recipes in this book may contain nuts. Always check the packaging before use.

CONTENTS

Introduction

If you cook nothing else, you could live exceptionally well on the rich variety of soups you will find in this easy-to-use book.

In many ways, soup is simple. It is either thin, as in consommés, or thick, either puréed or left chunky. This means it can be eaten at different mealtime occasions – thinner broths make perfect starters or healthy snacks, whilst more robust soups incorporating fish, meat or vegetables can be a meal in themselves. For even more diversity, some soups can even be served cold as well as hot – delicious on a hot summer's day.

There is a huge variety of ingredients and styles of soup, with many countries having their own traditional favourites – dishes that are firmly entrenched in that nation's culinary history. To name just a few, think of Spanish Gazpacho and Greek Avgolemono, Italian Minestrone and Ribollita, even Scottish Cullen Skink and Cock-a-leekie. Further east there are spicy Middle Eastern recipes and Indian lentil-based dhals. In the Far East, Thai flavours contrast with the blander Japanese Miso broth. Watch out for Bird's Nest Soup or Shark's Fin Soup when in China!

Soup-making is an exciting and challenging area of cookery. Don't be put off – all soups have three things in common, which helps make them simple to understand and explore.

Firstly, soup is very easy to make. Almost all soups start with frying up an onion with a tasty vegetable like leek or celery, to build a flavour base. You simply add an appropriate stock, together with the main ingredients of your choice, and cook for long enough to soften the textures and bring out the flavours. It really couldn't be simpler!

Secondly, home-made soup is healthy. You can guarantee the freshness and provenance of the raw ingredients, ensuring you are eating them in season and at the peak of their quality. There is usually very little fat involved and you can use the minimum amount of salt. This is why home-made soups are so much better for you than most commercially produced varieties.

Thirdly, soup is so convenient. It is ideal – fresh, or quickly defrosted from the freezer – for a quick meal or impromptu supper party at home, and it only needs a simple bowl for serving. It is easily portable too – just pack into a Thermos flask and you can enjoy a delicious cup of soup wherever and whenever you like.

Essential Equipment

The beauty of making soup is that it doesn't require lots of special equipment. All you will need to get started are a large, heavy-based saucepan and a few basic kitchen items – such as a sharp knife, a chopping board, a slotted spoon or ladle, a wooden spoon and a measuring jug – many of which you probably already have. Obviously, a blender or a food processor would be handy if you wish to make smooth soups, but a stick blender is a cheaper alternative. This useful piece of equipment allows you to blend your soup in the saucepan too, thus cutting down on washing up.

Key Ingredients

It is said that the base of a good soup is its stock but sometimes just water is good enough if you have lots of really fresh and tasty ingredients. You can make your own stock – you will find recipes for vegetable, fish, chicken and beef stocks on the following pages – but don't think you have to. There are many brands of stock cubes available. They come in meat, fish and vegetable flavours and can be very useful if you want to have a very specifically flavoured soup. Some stock cubes have a very concentrated flavour and are best used at half their strength so that they are not too salty. Bouillon powder is very handy as you can use it by the spoonful and adjust the flavour and saltiness according to taste. A newer way of using stock is to buy the bottles of liquid bouillon and use a spoonful at a time. They keep well in the fridge and add a good concentrated flavour. Finally, ready-made fresh stock is available from most large supermarkets, although it does tend to be quite expensive.

However, the best stock is the one you make yourself, using simple and wholesome ingredients. Here are a few tips:

- Use the freshest ingredients.
- When preparing the stock, make sure the water only simmers; boiling will make a cloudy stock.
- Always skim any scum from the top of the stock so that it will be clear.
- Make sure you strain the stock through a sieve to remove any unwanted vegetables and herbs.
- You can reduce the finished stock by boiling for a more concentrated flavour. This is particularly useful if you intend to freeze the stock, as you will have a smaller volume to store.
- Allow the stock to cool before use. This means that you will be able to completely remove any excess fat from the surface.

Vegetables play an important role in soups. Root vegetables, like parsnips, carrots and potatoes, are important for adding bulk. Bulbs like onions, shallots, garlic and leeks are always needed for flavour. Peas and beans can be puréed or just added to mixed soups to give colour and flavour. Squashes like courgettes and pumpkins are incredibly prolific when in season, so it is sensible to make soup with any excess. Vegetable fruits – this term covers tomatoes, avocados and sweet peppers – all make delicious summery-tasting soups. Always make sure that you use vegetables at the peak of their freshness.

Meat is found in various guises in soup-making. Bacon is particularly useful for adding flavour, as are sausages, especially the spicy ones. One advantage of the slow-cooking techniques employed in soup-making is that they enable cheaper cuts of meat to be used, resulting in melt-in-the-mouth tender meat and flavourful stock. Chickens – either whole or joints – can be used for stock and then the meat served separately or cut into smaller pieces and served as part of the soup.

Fish and seafood of all sorts can be used to make tasty soups and chowders – cod, salmon, squid, mussels, clams, prawns, crab, lobster and oysters. Sometimes a selection of fish is served together, as in the French classic, Bouillabaisse

Finally, don't forget dairy products! A little cream, crème fraîche or yogurt stirred in just before serving produces a soup with a lovely creamy texture. Using butter, instead of oil, will add flavour in the cooking too. Always keep a small piece of Cheddar or Parmesan cheese handy too for grating and sprinkling over soup just before serving.

Vegetable Stock

Makes: about 2 litres/3^1/$_2$ pints

Ingredients

2 tbsp sunflower oil
115 g/4 oz onion, finely chopped
40 g/1^1/$_2$ oz leek, finely chopped
115 g/4 oz carrots, finely chopped
4 celery sticks, finely chopped
85 g/3 oz fennel, finely chopped
1 small tomato, finely chopped
2.25 litres/4 pints water
1 bouquet garni

Heat the oil in a large saucepan. Add the onion and leek and cook over a low heat, stirring occasionally, for 5 minutes, until softened. Add the remaining vegetables, cover and cook for 10 minutes. Add the water and bouquet garni, bring to the boil and simmer for 20 minutes.

Strain the stock into a bowl, leave to cool, cover and store in the refrigerator. Use immediately or freeze in portions for up to 3 months.

Fish Stock

Makes: about 1.3 litres/2^1/$_4$ pints

Ingredients

650 g/1 lb 7 oz white fish heads, bones and
    trimmings, rinsed
1 onion, sliced
2 celery sticks, chopped
1 carrot, sliced
1 bay leaf
4 fresh parsley sprigs
4 black peppercorns
^{1}/$_2$ lemon, sliced
1.3 litres/2^1/$_4$ pints water
125 ml/4 fl oz dry white wine

Cut out and discard the gills from any fish heads, then place the heads, bones and trimmings in a saucepan. Add all the remaining ingredients and gradually bring to the boil, skimming off the scum that rises to the surface. Partially cover and simmer for 25 minutes.

Strain the stock without pressing down on the contents of the sieve. Leave to cool, cover and store in the refrigerator. Use immediately or freeze in portions for up to 3 months.

Chicken Stock

Makes: about 2.5 litres/4^1/$_2$ pints

Ingredients

1.3 kg/3 lb chicken wings and necks
2 onions, cut into wedges
4 litres/7 pints water
2 carrots, coarsely chopped
2 celery sticks, coarsely chopped
10 fresh parsley sprigs
4 fresh thyme sprigs
2 bay leaves
10 black peppercorns

Put the chicken wings and necks and the onions in a large saucepan and cook over a low heat, stirring frequently, until lightly browned.

Add the water and stir well to scrape off any sediment from the base of the pan. Gradually bring to the boil, skimming off the scum that rises to the surface. Add all the remaining ingredients, partially cover and simmer for 3 hours.

Strain the stock into a bowl, leave to cool, cover and store in the refrigerator. When cold, remove and discard the layer of fat from the surface. Use immediately or freeze in portions for up to 6 months.

Beef Stock

Makes: about 1.7 litres/3 pints

Ingredients

1 kg/2 lb 4 oz beef marrow bones, sawn into
    7.5-cm/3-inch pieces
650 g/1 lb 7 oz stewing steak in a single piece
2.8 litres/5 pints water
4 cloves
2 onions, halved
2 celery sticks, coarsely chopped
8 black peppercorns
1 bouquet garni

Place the bones in the base of a large saucepan and put the meat on top. Add the water and gradually bring to the boil, skimming off the scum that rises to the surface.

Press a clove into each onion half and add to the pan with the celery, peppercorns and bouquet garni. Partially cover and simmer for 3 hours. Remove the meat and simmer for 1 hour more.

Strain the stock into a bowl, leave to cool, cover and store in the refrigerator. When cold, remove and discard the layer of fat from the surface. Use immediately or freeze in portions for up to 6 months.

1

Classic Soups

In this chapter you will find all your old favourites, like Tomato Soup and Chicken Noodle Soup, along with some more sophisticated combinations, such as Creamy Carrot & Parsnip Soup and Clam & Corn Chowder. There is nothing more welcoming than returning home to the aroma of freshly-made soup and these familiar favourites are sure to be a hit with all the family.

Tomato Soup

Melt half the butter in a saucepan. Add the onion and cook over a low heat, stirring occasionally, for 5–6 minutes until softened. Add the tomatoes and bay leaf and cook, stirring occasionally, for 15 minutes, or until pulpy.

Meanwhile, melt the remaining butter in another saucepan. Add the flour and cook, stirring constantly, for 1 minute. Remove the pan from the heat and gradually stir in the milk. Return to the heat, season with salt and pepper and bring to the boil, stirring constantly. Continue to cook, stirring, until smooth and thickened.

When the tomatoes are pulpy, remove the pan from the heat. Discard the bay leaf and pour the tomato mixture into a blender or food processor. Process until smooth, then push through a sieve into a clean saucepan. Bring the tomato mixture to the boil, then gradually stir it into the milk mixture. Season to taste with salt and pepper. Ladle into warmed bowls, garnish with basil and serve immediately.

SERVES 4

55 g/2 oz butter

1 small onion, finely chopped

450 g/1 lb tomatoes, coarsely chopped

1 bay leaf

3 tbsp plain flour

600 ml/1 pint milk

salt and pepper

sprigs of fresh basil, to garnish

Chunky Vegetable Soup

Put the carrots, onion, garlic, potatoes, celery, mushrooms, tomatoes and stock into a large saucepan. Stir in the bay leaf and herbs. Bring to the boil, then reduce the heat, cover and simmer for 25 minutes.

Add the sweetcorn and cabbage and return to the boil. Reduce the heat, cover and simmer for 5 minutes, or until the vegetables are tender. Remove and discard the bay leaf. Season to taste with pepper.

Ladle into warmed bowls, garnish with basil, if using, and serve immediately.

SERVES 6

2 carrots, sliced

1 onion, diced

1 garlic clove, crushed

350 g/12 oz new potatoes, diced

2 celery sticks, sliced

115 g/4 oz closed-cup mushrooms, quartered

400 g/14 oz canned chopped tomatoes

600 ml/1 pint vegetable stock

1 bay leaf

1 tsp dried mixed herbs or 1 tbsp chopped fresh mixed herbs

85 g/3 oz sweetcorn kernels, frozen or canned, drained

55 g/2 oz green cabbage, shredded

freshly ground black pepper

sprigs of fresh basil, to garnish (optional)

Minestrone

Heat the oil in a large saucepan. Add the garlic, onions and Parma ham and cook over a medium heat, stirring, for 3 minutes, until slightly softened. Add the red and orange peppers and the chopped tomatoes and cook for a further 2 minutes, stirring. Stir in the stock, then add the celery. Drain and add the borlotti beans along with the cabbage, peas and parsley. Season with salt and pepper. Bring to the boil, then lower the heat and simmer for 30 minutes.

Add the vermicelli to the pan. Cook for a further 10–12 minutes, or according to the instructions on the packet. Remove from the heat and ladle into serving bowls. Garnish with freshly grated Parmesan and serve immediately.

SERVES 4

2 tbsp olive oil

2 garlic cloves, chopped

2 red onions, chopped

75 g/2³/₄ oz Parma ham, sliced

1 red pepper, deseeded and chopped

1 orange pepper, deseeded and chopped

400 g/14 oz canned chopped tomatoes

1 litre/1³/₄ pints vegetable stock

1 celery stick, chopped

400 g/14 oz canned borlotti beans

100 g/3¹/₂ oz green leafy cabbage, shredded

75 g/2³/₄ oz frozen peas, defrosted

1 tbsp chopped fresh parsley

75 g/2³/₄ oz dried vermicelli

salt and pepper

freshly grated Parmesan cheese, to garnish

Leek & Potato Soup

Melt the butter in a large saucepan over a medium heat, add the onion, leeks and potatoes and sauté gently for 2–3 minutes, until soft but not brown. Pour in the stock, bring to the boil, then reduce the heat and simmer, covered, for 15 minutes.

Transfer the mixture to a food processor or blender and process until smooth. Return to the rinsed-out saucepan.

Heat the soup, season with salt and pepper to taste and serve in warmed bowls, swirled with the cream, if using, and garnished with chives.

SERVES 4–6

55 g/2 oz butter

1 onion, chopped

3 leeks, sliced

225 g/8 oz potatoes, cut into
 2-cm/^{3}/$_4$-inch cubes

850 ml/1^1/$_2$ pints vegetable stock

salt and pepper

150 ml/5 fl oz single cream,
 to serve (optional)

2 tbsp snipped fresh chives,
 to garnish

French Onion Soup

Heat the oil in a large, heavy-based saucepan over a medium-low heat, add the onions and cook, stirring occasionally, for 10 minutes, or until they are just beginning to brown. Stir in the chopped garlic, sugar and chopped thyme, then reduce the heat and cook, stirring occasionally, for 30 minutes, or until the onions are golden brown.

Sprinkle in the flour and cook, stirring constantly, for 1–2 minutes. Stir in the wine. Gradually stir in the stock and bring to the boil, skimming off any scum that rises to the surface, then reduce the heat and simmer for 45 minutes.

Meanwhile, preheat the grill to medium. Toast the bread on both sides under the grill, then rub the toast with the cut edges of the halved garlic clove.

Ladle the soup into 6 flameproof bowls set on a baking tray. Float a piece of toast in each bowl and divide the grated cheese between them. Place under the grill for 2–3 minutes, or until the cheese has just melted. Garnish with thyme sprigs and serve at once.

SERVES 6

3 tbsp olive oil

675 g/1 lb 8 oz onions, thinly sliced

4 garlic cloves, 3 chopped and
   1 peeled and halved

1 tsp sugar

2 tsp chopped fresh thyme, plus
   extra sprigs to garnish

2 tbsp plain flour

125 ml/4 fl oz dry white wine

2 litres/3^1/$_2$ pints vegetable stock

6 slices French bread

300 g/10^1/$_2$ oz Gruyère cheese,
   grated

Creamy Mushroom & Tarragon Soup

Melt half the butter in a large saucepan. Add the onion and cook gently for 10 minutes, until soft. Add the remaining butter and the mushrooms and cook for 5 minutes, or until the mushrooms are browned.

Stir in the stock and tarragon, bring to the boil, then reduce the heat and leave to simmer gently for 20 minutes. Transfer to a food processor or blender and process until smooth. Return the soup to the rinsed-out saucepan.

Stir in the crème fraîche and add salt and pepper to taste. Reheat the soup gently until hot. Ladle into warmed serving bowls and garnish with chopped tarragon. Serve immediately.

SERVES 4–6

50 g/1^3/$_4$ oz butter

1 onion, chopped

700 g/1 lb 9 oz button mushrooms, coarsely chopped

850 ml/1^1/$_2$ pints vegetable stock

3 tbsp chopped fresh tarragon, plus extra to garnish

150 ml/5 fl oz crème fraîche

salt and pepper

Cauliflower Soup

Heat the oil and butter in a large saucepan and fry the onion and leeks for 10 minutes, stirring frequently, taking care not to allow the vegetables to colour.

Cut the cauliflower into florets and cut the stalk into small pieces. Add to the pan and sauté with the other vegetables for 2–3 minutes.

Add the stock and bring to the boil, cover and simmer over a medium heat for 20 minutes.

Pour the soup into a food processor or blender, process until smooth and return to the rinsed-out saucepan.

Heat the soup through, season to taste with salt and pepper and serve in warmed bowls topped with a spoonful of grated cheese and a drizzle of extra virgin olive oil.

SERVES 6

1 tbsp olive oil

25 g/1 oz butter

1 large onion, coarsely chopped

2 leeks, sliced

1 large cauliflower

900 ml/1½ pints vegetable stock

salt and pepper

finely grated Cheddar cheese and
    extra virgin olive oil, to serve

Watercress Soup

Remove the leaves from the stalks of the watercress and set aside. Roughly chop the stalks.

Melt the butter in a large saucepan over a medium heat, add the onions and cook for 4–5 minutes, until soft. Do not brown.

Add the potatoes to the saucepan and mix well with the onions. Add the watercress stalks and the stock.

Bring to the boil, then reduce the heat, cover and simmer for 15–20 minutes, until the potato is soft.

Add the watercress leaves and stir in to heat through. Remove from the heat and transfer to a food processor or blender. Process until smooth and return the soup to the rinsed-out saucepan. Reheat and season with salt and pepper to taste, adding a good grating of nutmeg if using.

Serve in warmed bowls with the crème fraîche spooned on top and an extra grating of nutmeg, if desired.

SERVES 4

2 bunches of watercress (about
   200 g/7 oz), thoroughly cleaned
40 g/1^{1}/$_{2}$ oz butter
2 onions, chopped
225 g/8 oz potatoes, coarsely
   chopped
1.2 litres/2 pints vegetable stock or
   water
whole nutmeg, for grating (optional)
salt and pepper
125 ml/4 fl oz crème fraîche,
   to serve

Asparagus Soup

Wash and trim the asparagus, discarding the woody part of the stem. Cut the remainder into short lengths, reserving a few tips for garnish. Fine asparagus does not need to be trimmed.

Cook the tips in the minimum of boiling salted water for 5–10 minutes. Drain and set aside.

Put the asparagus in a saucepan with the stock, bring to the boil, cover and simmer for about 20 minutes, until soft. Drain and reserve the stock.

Melt the butter or margarine in a saucepan. Add the onion and cook over a low heat until soft, but only barely coloured. Stir in the flour and cook for 1 minute, then gradually whisk in the reserved stock and bring to the boil.

Simmer for 2–3 minutes, until thickened, then stir in the cooked asparagus, coriander, lemon juice and salt and pepper to taste. Simmer for 10 minutes. Remove from the heat and allow to cool a little. Transfer to a food processor or blender and process until smooth.

Pour into a clean pan, add the milk and reserved asparagus tips and bring to the boil. Simmer for 2 minutes. Stir in the cream, reheat gently and serve.

SERVES 6

1 bunch asparagus, about 350 g/
    12 oz, or 2 packs fine asparagus,
    about 150 g/5$^{1}/_{2}$ oz each
700 ml/1$^{1}/_{4}$ pints vegetable stock
55 g/2 oz butter or margarine
1 onion, chopped
3 tbsp plain flour
$^{1}/_{4}$ tsp ground coriander
1 tbsp lemon juice
450 ml/16 fl oz milk
4–6 tbsp double cream or
    single cream
salt and pepper

Creamy Carrot & Parsnip Soup

Melt the butter in a large saucepan over a low heat. Add the onion and cook, stirring, for 3 minutes, until slightly softened. Add the carrots and parsnips, cover the pan and cook, stirring occasionally, for about 15 minutes, until the vegetables have softened a little. Stir in the ginger, orange rind and stock. Bring to the boil, then reduce the heat, cover the pan and simmer for 30–35 minutes, until the vegetables are tender. Remove from the heat and leave to cool for 10 minutes.

Transfer the soup to a food processor or blender and process until smooth. Return the soup to the rinsed-out saucepan, stir in the cream and season well with salt and pepper. Warm through gently over a low heat.

Remove from the heat and ladle into soup bowls. Garnish each bowl with pepper and a sprig of coriander and serve.

SERVES 4

4 tbsp butter

1 large onion, chopped

450 g/1 lb carrots, chopped

2 large parsnips, chopped

1 tbsp grated fresh root ginger

1 tsp grated orange rind

600 ml/1 pint vegetable stock

125 ml/4 fl oz single cream

salt and pepper

sprigs of fresh coriander, to garnish

Roasted Squash, Sweet Potato & Garlic Soup

Preheat the oven to 190°C/375°F/Gas Mark 5.

Cut the sweet potato, squash and shallots in half lengthways, through to the stem end. Scoop the seeds out of the squash. Brush the cut sides with the oil.

Put the vegetables, cut-side down, in a shallow roasting tin. Add the garlic cloves. Roast in the preheated oven for about 40 minutes, until tender and light brown.

When cool, scoop the flesh from the potato and squash halves and put in a saucepan with the shallots. Remove the garlic peel and add the soft insides to the other vegetables.

Add the stock and a pinch of salt. Bring just to the boil, reduce the heat and simmer, partially covered, for about 30 minutes, stirring occasionally, until the vegetables are very tender.

Allow the soup to cool slightly, then transfer to a food processor or blender and process until smooth, working in batches, if necessary. (If using a food processor, strain off the cooking liquid and reserve. Process the soup solids with enough cooking liquid to moisten them, then combine with the remaining liquid.)

Return the soup to the rinsed-out saucepan and stir in the cream. Season to taste with salt and pepper, then simmer for 5–10 minutes until completely heated through. Ladle into warmed serving bowls, garnish with pepper and snipped chives and serve.

SERVES 6–8

1 sweet potato, about 350 g/12 oz

1 acorn squash

4 shallots

2 tbsp olive oil

5–6 garlic cloves, unpeeled

850 ml/1¹/₂ pints chicken stock

125 ml/4 fl oz single cream

salt and pepper

snipped chives, to garnish

Spiced Pumpkin Soup

Heat the oil in a saucepan over a medium heat. Add the onion and garlic and cook, stirring, for about 4 minutes, until slightly softened. Add the ginger, chilli, coriander, bay leaf and pumpkin and cook for another 3 minutes.

Pour in the stock and bring to the boil. Using a slotted spoon, skim any scum from the surface. Reduce the heat and simmer gently, stirring occasionally, for about 25 minutes, or until the pumpkin is tender. Remove from the heat, take out the bay leaf and leave to cool a little.

Transfer the soup to a food processor or blender and process until smooth (you may have to do this in batches). Return the mixture to the rinsed-out pan and season to taste with salt and pepper. Reheat gently, stirring. Remove from the heat, pour into 4 warmed soup bowls, garnish each one with a swirl of cream and serve.

SERVES 4

2 tbsp olive oil

1 onion, chopped

1 garlic clove, chopped

1 tbsp chopped fresh root ginger

1 small red chilli, deseeded and
    finely chopped

2 tbsp chopped fresh coriander

1 bay leaf

1 kg/2 lb 4 oz pumpkin, peeled,
    deseeded and diced

600 ml/1 pint vegetable stock

salt and pepper

single cream, to garnish

Winter Warmer Red Lentil Soup

Put the lentils, onion, vegetables, garlic, stock and paprika into a large saucepan. Bring to the boil and boil rapidly for 10 minutes. Reduce the heat, cover and simmer for 20 minutes, or until the lentils and vegetables are tender.

Leave the soup to cool slightly, then purée in small batches in a food processor or blender. Process until the mixture is smooth.

Return the soup to the rinsed-out saucepan and heat through thoroughly. Season to taste with pepper.

Ladle the soup into warmed bowls, garnish with snipped chives and serve.

SERVES 6

225 g/8 oz dried red split lentils

1 red onion, diced

2 large carrots, sliced

1 celery stick, sliced

1 parsnip, diced

1 garlic clove, crushed

1.2 litres/2 pints vegetable stock

2 tsp paprika

pepper

1 tbsp snipped fresh chives, to garnish

Split Pea & Ham Soup

Rinse the peas under cold running water. Put in a saucepan and cover generously with water. Bring to the boil and boil for 3 minutes, skimming off the scum from the surface. Drain the peas.

Heat the oil in a large saucepan over a medium heat. Add the onion and cook for 3–4 minutes, stirring occasionally, until just softened.

Add the carrot and celery and continue cooking for 2 minutes. Add the peas, pour over the stock and water and stir to combine.

Bring just to the boil and stir the ham into the soup. Add the thyme, marjoram and bay leaf. Reduce the heat, cover and cook gently for 1–1½ hours, until the ingredients are very soft. Remove the bay leaf.

Taste and adjust the seasoning. Ladle into warmed soup bowls and serve.

SERVES 6–8

500 g/1 lb 2 oz split green peas

1 tbsp olive oil

1 large onion, finely chopped

1 large carrot, finely chopped

1 celery stick, finely chopped

1 litre/1¾ pints chicken or vegetable stock

1 litre/1¾ pints water

225 g/8 oz lean smoked ham, finely diced

¼ tsp dried thyme

¼ tsp dried marjoram

1 bay leaf

salt and pepper

Cream of Chicken Soup

Melt the butter in a large saucepan over a medium heat. Add the shallots and cook, stirring, for 3 minutes, until slightly softened. Add the leek and cook for a further 5 minutes, stirring. Add the chicken, stock and herbs, and season with salt and pepper. Bring to the boil, then lower the heat and simmer for 25 minutes, until the chicken is tender and cooked through. Remove from the heat and leave to cool for 10 minutes.

Transfer the soup to a food processor or blender and process until smooth (you may need to do this in batches). Return the soup to the rinsed-out pan and warm over a low heat for 5 minutes.

Stir in the cream and cook for a further 2 minutes, then remove from the heat and ladle into serving bowls. Garnish with sprigs of thyme and serve immediately.

SERVES 4

3 tbsp butter

4 shallots, chopped

1 leek, sliced

450 g/1 lb skinless chicken breasts, chopped

600 ml/1 pint chicken stock

1 tbsp chopped fresh parsley

1 tbsp chopped fresh thyme, plus extra sprigs to garnish

175 ml/6 fl oz double cream

salt and pepper

Chicken Noodle Soup

Place the chicken breasts in a large saucepan, add the water and bring to a simmer. Cook for 25–30 minutes. Skim any scum from the surface if necessary. Remove the chicken from the stock and keep warm.

Continue to simmer the stock, add the carrots and vermicelli and cook for 4–5 minutes.

Thinly slice or shred the chicken breasts and place in warmed serving dishes.

Season the soup to taste with salt and pepper and pour over the chicken. Serve at once garnished with the tarragon.

SERVES 4–6

2 skinless chicken breasts

1.2 litres/2 pints water or chicken stock

3 carrots, peeled and sliced into 5-mm/$\frac{1}{4}$-inch slices

85 g/3 oz vermicelli (or other small noodles)

salt and pepper

fresh tarragon leaves, to garnish

Chicken & Rice Soup

Put the stock in a large saucepan and add the carrots, celery and leek. Bring to the boil, reduce the heat to low and simmer gently, partially covered, for 10 minutes.

Stir in the petit pois, rice and chicken and continue cooking for a further 10–15 minutes, or until the vegetables are tender.

Add the chopped tarragon and parsley, then taste and adjust the seasoning, adding salt and pepper as needed.

Ladle the soup into warmed bowls, garnish with parsley and serve.

SERVES 4

1.5 litres/2^3/$_4$ pints chicken stock

2 small carrots, very thinly sliced

1 celery stick, finely diced

1 baby leek, halved lengthways and thinly sliced

115 g/4 oz petit pois, defrosted if frozen

175 g/6 oz cooked rice

150 g/5^1/$_2$ oz cooked chicken, sliced

2 tsp chopped fresh tarragon

1 tbsp chopped fresh parsley

salt and pepper

sprigs of fresh parsley, to garnish

Beef & Vegetable Soup

Place the pearl barley in a large saucepan. Pour over the stock and add the mixed herbs. Bring to the boil, cover and simmer gently over a low heat for 10 minutes.

Meanwhile, trim any fat from the beef and cut the meat into thin strips.

Skim away any scum that has risen to the top of the stock with a flat ladle.

Add the beef, carrot, leek, onion and celery to the pan. Bring back to the boil, cover and simmer for about 1 hour or until the pearl barley, beef and vegetables are just tender.

Skim away any remaining scum that has risen to the top of the soup with a flat ladle. Blot the surface with absorbent kitchen paper to remove any fat. Adjust the seasoning according to taste.

Ladle the soup into warmed bowls, garnish with chopped parsley and serve hot.

SERVES 4

55 g/2 oz pearl barley

1.2 litres/2 pints beef stock

1 tsp dried mixed herbs

225 g/8 oz lean rump or sirloin
   beef

1 large carrot, diced

1 leek, shredded

1 medium onion, chopped

2 celery sticks, sliced

salt and pepper

2 tbsp chopped fresh parsley, to
   garnish

Clam & Corn Chowder

If using fresh clams, wash under cold running water. Discard any with broken shells or any that refuse to close when tapped. Put the clams into a heavy-based saucepan with the wine. Cover tightly, set over a medium-high heat and cook for 2–4 minutes, or until they open, shaking the pan occasionally. Discard any that remain closed. Remove the clams from the shells and strain the cooking liquid through a very fine mesh sieve; reserve both. If using canned clams, drain and rinse well.

Melt the butter in a large saucepan over a medium-low heat. Add the onion and carrot and cook for 3–4 minutes, stirring frequently, until the onion is softened. Stir in the flour and continue cooking for 2 minutes.

Slowly add about half the stock and stir well, scraping the bottom of the pan to mix in the flour. Pour in the remaining stock and the reserved clam cooking liquid, or the water if using canned clams, and bring just to the boil, stirring.

Add the potatoes, sweetcorn and milk and stir to combine. Reduce the heat and simmer gently, partially covered, for about 20 minutes, stirring occasionally, until all the vegetables are tender.

Chop the clams, if large. Stir in the clams and continue cooking for about 5 minutes until heated through. Taste and adjust the seasoning, if needed.

Ladle the soup into bowls and sprinkle with parsley.

SERVES 4

750 g/1 lb 10 oz clams, or 280 g/
    10 oz canned clams
2 tbsp dry white wine (if using
    fresh clams)
4 tsp butter
1 large onion, finely chopped
1 small carrot, finely diced
3 tbsp plain flour
300 ml/10 fl oz fish stock
200 ml/7 fl oz water (if using
    canned clams)
450 g/1 lb potatoes, diced
125 g/4 oz sweetcorn, thawed if
    frozen
450 ml/16 fl oz full-fat milk
salt and pepper
chopped fresh parsley, to garnish

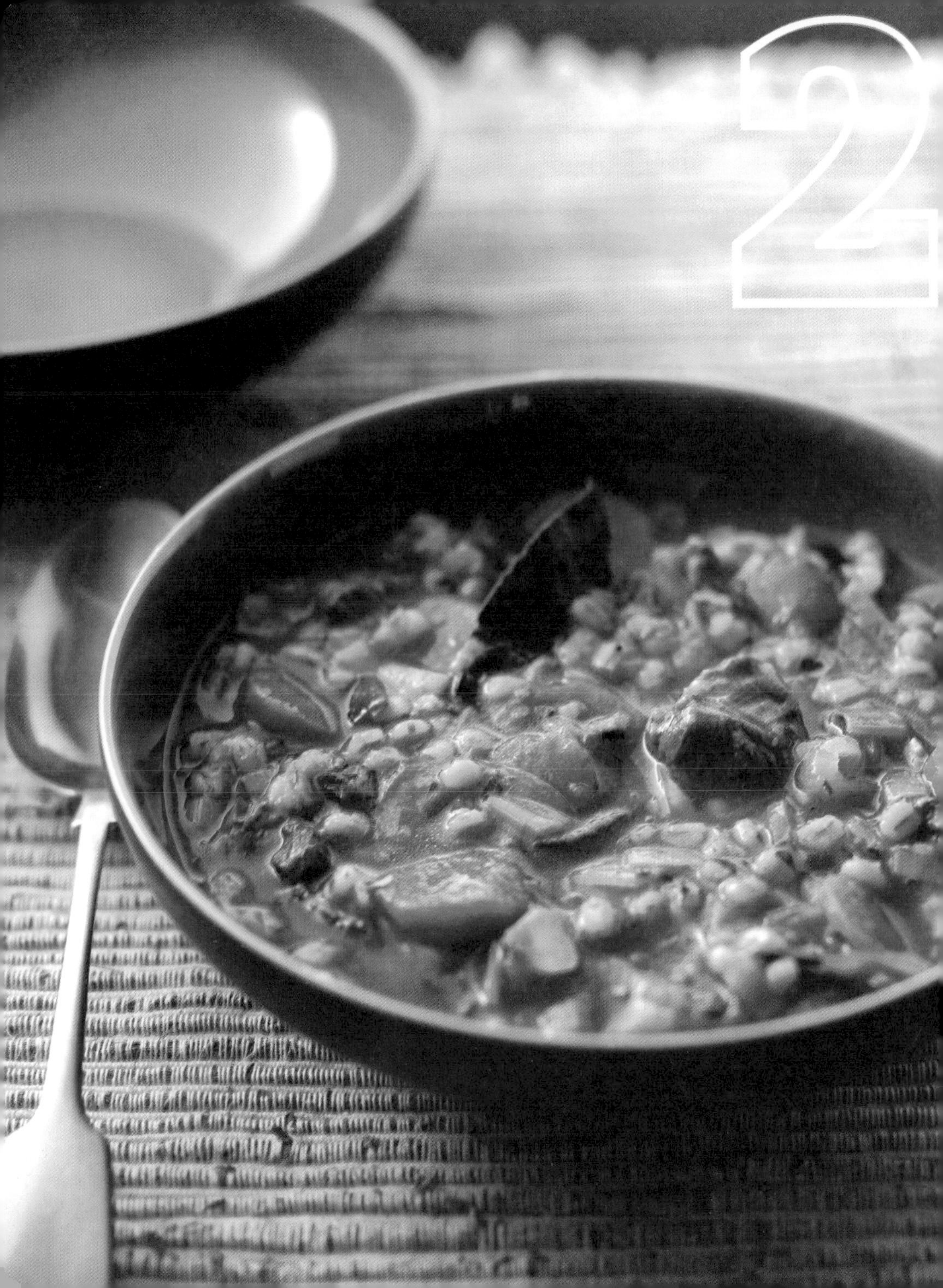
2

Hearty Soups

These nourishing and satisfying bowlfuls are ideal comfort food on a cold winter's day. Try Tuscan Bean Soup or Mushroom & Barley Soup – both are meals in themselves, but those with especially large appetites can serve them with chunks of fresh bread. These soups are perfect for filling the gap and keeping you going, however hectic your day might be.

Vegetable Soup with Pesto

Heat the olive oil in a large saucepan over a medium-low heat. Add the onion and leek and cook for 5 minutes, stirring occasionally, until the onion softens. Add the celery, carrot and garlic and cook, covered, for a further 5 minutes, stirring frequently.

Add the water, potato, parsnip, kohlrabi and green beans. Bring to the boil, reduce the heat to low and simmer, covered, for 5 minutes.

Add the peas, courgettes and flageolet beans, and season generously with salt and pepper. Cover again and simmer for about 25 minutes until all the vegetables are tender.

Meanwhile, make the pesto. Put the garlic, basil and Parmesan in a food processor with the olive oil and process until smooth, scraping down the sides as necessary. Alternatively, pound together using a pestle and mortar.

Add the spinach to the soup and simmer for a further 5 minutes. Taste and adjust the seasoning and stir about a tablespoon of the pesto into the soup. Ladle into warmed bowls and serve with the remaining pesto.

SERVES 6

1 tbsp olive oil
1 onion, finely chopped
1 large leek, thinly sliced
1 celery stick, thinly sliced
1 carrot, quartered and thinly sliced
1 garlic clove, finely chopped
1.4 litres/2^1/$_2$ pints water
1 potato, diced
1 parsnip, finely diced
1 small kohlrabi or turnip, diced
150 g/5^1/$_2$ oz green beans,
   cut in small pieces
150 g/5^1/$_2$ oz fresh or frozen peas
2 small courgettes, quartered
   lengthways and sliced
400 g/14 oz canned flageolet beans,
   drained and rinsed
100 g/3^1/$_2$ oz spinach leaves,
   cut into thin ribbons
salt and pepper

pesto

1 large garlic clove, very finely
   chopped
15 g/^{1}/$_2$ oz basil leaves
75 g/2^3/$_4$ oz Parmesan cheese,
   grated
4 tbsp extra virgin olive oil

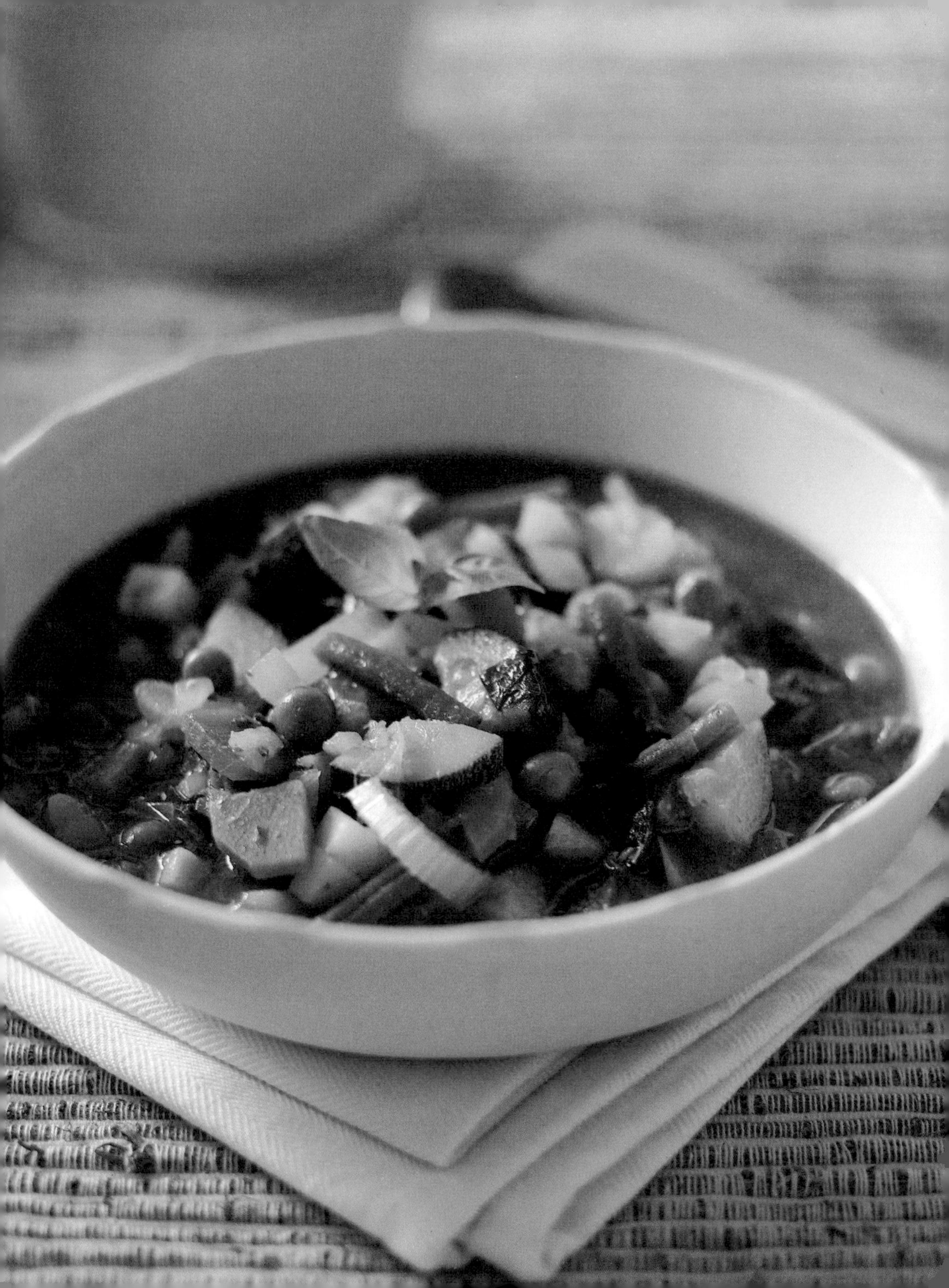

Roasted Mediterranean Vegetable Soup

Preheat the oven to 190°C/375°F/Gas Mark 5.

Brush a large shallow baking dish with olive oil. Laying them cut-side down, arrange the tomatoes, peppers, courgettes and aubergine in one layer (use two dishes, if necessary). Tuck the garlic cloves and onion pieces into the gaps and drizzle the vegetables with the remaining olive oil. Season lightly with salt and pepper and sprinkle with the thyme.

Place in the preheated oven and bake, uncovered, for 30–35 minutes, or until soft and browned around the edges. Leave to cool, then scrape out the aubergine flesh and remove the skin from the peppers.

Working in batches, put the aubergine and pepper flesh, together with the tomatoes, courgettes, garlic and onion, into a food processor and chop to the consistency of salsa or pickle; do not purée. Alternatively, place in a bowl and chop together with a knife.

Combine the stock and chopped vegetable mixture in a saucepan and simmer over a medium heat for 20-30 minutes, until all the vegetables are tender and the flavours have completely blended.

Stir in the cream and simmer over a low heat for about 5 minutes, stirring occasionally until hot. Taste and adjust the seasoning, if necessary. Ladle the soup into warmed bowls, garnish with basil and serve.

SERVES 6

3 tbsp olive oil

700 g/1 lb 9 oz ripe tomatoes, skinned, cored and halved

3 large yellow peppers, deseeded and halved

3 courgettes, halved lengthways

1 small aubergine, halved lengthways

4 garlic cloves, halved

2 onions, cut into eighths

pinch of dried thyme

1 litre/$1^3/4$ pints chicken, vegetable or meat stock

125 ml/4 fl oz single cream

salt and pepper

shredded basil leaves, to garnish

Ribollita

Heat the oil in a large saucepan and cook the onions, carrots and celery for 10–15 minutes, stirring frequently. Add the garlic, thyme and salt and pepper to taste. Continue to cook for a further 1–2 minutes, until the vegetables are golden and caramelized.

Add the cannellini beans to the pan and pour in the tomatoes. Add enough of the water to cover the vegetables.

Bring to the boil and simmer for 20 minutes. Add the parsley and cavolo nero and cook for a further 5 minutes.

Stir in the bread and add a little more water, if needed. The soup should be thick.

Taste and adjust the seasoning, if needed. Ladle into warmed serving bowls and serve hot, drizzled with extra virgin olive oil.

SERVES 4

3 tbsp olive oil

2 medium red onions, coarsely chopped

3 carrots, sliced

3 celery sticks, coarsely chopped

3 garlic cloves, chopped

1 tbsp chopped fresh thyme

400 g/14 oz canned cannellini beans, drained and rinsed

400 g/14 oz canned chopped tomatoes

600 ml/1 pint water or vegetable stock

2 tbsp chopped fresh parsley

500 g/1 lb 2 oz cavolo nero or Savoy cabbage, trimmed and sliced

1 small day-old ciabatta loaf, torn into small pieces

salt and pepper

extra virgin olive oil, to serve

Vegetable & Corn Chowder

Heat the oil in a large saucepan. Add the onion, pepper, garlic and potato and cook over a low heat, stirring frequently, for 2–3 minutes.

Stir in the flour and cook, stirring for 30 seconds. Gradually stir in the milk and stock.

Add the broccoli and sweetcorn. Bring the mixture to the boil, stirring constantly, then reduce the heat and simmer for about 20 minutes, or until all the vegetables are tender.

Stir in 50 g/1¾ oz of the cheese until it melts.

Season to taste with salt and pepper and spoon the chowder into warmed serving bowls. Garnish with the remaining cheese and the coriander and serve.

SERVES 4

1 tbsp vegetable oil

1 red onion, diced

1 red pepper, deseeded and diced

3 garlic cloves, crushed

1 large potato, diced

2 tbsp plain flour

600 ml/1 pint milk

300 ml/10 fl oz vegetable stock

50 g/1¾ oz broccoli florets

300 g/10½ oz canned
   sweetcorn, drained

75 g/2¾ oz Cheddar cheese,
   grated

salt and pepper

1 tbsp chopped fresh coriander,
   to garnish

Mushroom & Barley Soup

Rinse the pearl barley and drain. Bring 450 ml/16 fl oz of the stock to the boil in a small saucepan. Add the bay leaf and, if the stock is unsalted, add a large pinch of salt. Stir in the pearl barley, reduce the heat, cover and simmer for 40 minutes.

Melt the butter in a large frying pan over a medium heat. Add the mushrooms and season with salt and pepper. Cook for about 8 minutes until they are golden brown, stirring occasionally at first, then more often after they start to colour. Remove the mushrooms from the heat.

Heat the oil in a large saucepan over a medium heat and add the onion and carrots. Cover and cook for about 3 minutes, stirring frequently, until the onion is softened.

Add the remaining stock and bring to the boil. Stir in the barley with its cooking liquid and add the mushrooms. Reduce the heat, cover and simmer gently for about 20 minutes, or until the carrots are tender, stirring occasionally.

Stir in the tarragon and parsley. Taste and adjust the seasoning, if necessary. Ladle into warmed bowls, garnish with fresh parsley and tarragon and serve.

SERVES 4

55 g/2 oz pearl barley

1.5 litres/$2^3/_4$ pints chicken or vegetable stock

1 bay leaf

1 tbsp butter

350 g/12 oz mushrooms, thinly sliced

1 tsp olive oil

1 onion, finely chopped

2 carrots, thinly sliced

1 tbsp chopped fresh tarragon, plus extra to garnish

1 tbsp chopped fresh parsley, plus extra to garnish

salt and pepper

Kidney Bean, Pumpkin & Tomato Soup

Pick over the beans, cover generously with cold water and leave to soak for 6 hours or overnight. Drain the beans, put in a saucepan and add enough cold water to cover by 5 cm/2 inches. Bring to the boil and boil for 10 minutes. Drain and rinse well.

Heat the oil in a large saucepan over a medium heat. Add the onions, cover and cook for 3–4 minutes, until they are just softened, stirring occasionally. Add the garlic, celery and carrot, and continue cooking for 2 minutes.

Add the water, drained beans, tomato purée, thyme, oregano, cumin and bay leaf. When the mixture begins to bubble, reduce the heat to low. Cover and simmer gently for 1 hour, stirring occasionally.

Stir in the tomatoes, pumpkin and chilli purée and continue simmering for a further hour, or until the beans and pumpkin are tender, stirring from time to time.

Season to taste with salt and pepper and stir in a little more chilli purée, if liked. Ladle the soup into bowls, garnish with coriander and serve.

SERVES 4–6

250 g/9 oz dried kidney beans

1 tbsp olive oil

2 onions, finely chopped

4 garlic cloves, finely chopped

1 celery stick, thinly sliced

1 carrot, halved and thinly sliced

1.2 litres/2 pints water

2 tsp tomato purée

$1/8$ tsp dried thyme

$1/8$ tsp dried oregano

$1/8$ tsp ground cumin

1 bay leaf

400 g/14 oz canned chopped tomatoes

250 g/9 oz peeled pumpkin flesh, diced

$1/4$ tsp chilli purée, or to taste

salt and pepper

fresh coriander leaves, to garnish

Tuscan Bean Soup

Place half the cannellini and half the borlotti beans in a food processor with half the chicken stock and process until smooth. Pour into a large, heavy-based saucepan and add the remaining beans. Stir in enough of the remaining stock to achieve the consistency you like, then bring to the boil.

Add the pasta and return to the boil, then reduce the heat and cook for 15 minutes, or until just tender.

Meanwhile, heat 3 tablespoons of the oil in a small frying pan. Add the garlic and cook, stirring constantly, for 2–3 minutes, or until golden. Stir the garlic into the soup with the parsley.

Season to taste with salt and pepper and ladle into warmed soup bowls. Drizzle with the remaining olive oil to taste and serve immediately.

SERVES 6

300 g/10^1/$_2$ oz canned cannellini beans, drained and rinsed

300 g/10^1/$_2$ oz canned borlotti beans, drained and rinsed

600 ml/1 pint chicken or vegetable stock

115 g/4 oz dried conchigliette or other small pasta shapes

4 tbsp olive oil

2 garlic cloves, very finely chopped

3 tbsp chopped fresh flat-leaf parsley

salt and pepper

Garlic & Chickpea Soup

Heat half the oil in a large, heavy-based saucepan. Add the garlic and cook over a low heat, stirring frequently, for 2 minutes. Add the chickpeas to the saucepan with the water, cumin and ground coriander. Bring to the boil, then reduce the heat and simmer for $2^1/2$ hours, or until tender.

Meanwhile, heat the remaining oil in a separate saucepan. Add the carrots, onions and celery, cover and cook over a medium-low heat, stirring occasionally, for 20 minutes.

Stir the vegetable mixture into the saucepan of chickpeas. Transfer about half the soup to a food processor or blender and process until smooth. Return the purée to the saucepan, add about half the lemon juice and stir. Taste and add more lemon juice as required. Season to taste with salt and pepper.

Ladle into warmed bowls, sprinkle with the fresh coriander and serve.

SERVES 4

8 tbsp olive oil

12 garlic cloves, very finely chopped

350 g / 12 oz chickpeas, soaked overnight in cold water and drained

2.5 litres / $4^1/2$ pints water

1 tsp ground cumin

1 tsp ground coriander

2 carrots, very finely chopped

2 onions, very finely chopped

6 celery sticks, very finely chopped

juice of 1 lemon

salt and pepper

4 tbsp chopped fresh coriander

Sweetcorn, Potato & Cheese Soup

To make the croûtons, cut the crusts off the bread slices, then cut the remaining bread into 5-mm/¼-inch squares. Heat the olive oil in a heavy-based frying pan and add the bread cubes. Cook, tossing and stirring constantly, until evenly coloured. Drain the croûtons thoroughly on kitchen paper and reserve.

Melt the butter in a large, heavy-based saucepan. Add the shallots and cook over a low heat, stirring occasionally, for 5 minutes, or until softened. Add the potatoes and cook, stirring, for 2 minutes.

Sprinkle in the flour and cook, stirring, for 1 minute. Remove the saucepan from the heat and stir in the white wine, then gradually stir in the milk. Return the saucepan to the heat and bring to the boil, stirring constantly, then reduce the heat and simmer.

Stir in the sweetcorn kernels, grated cheese, chopped sage and cream and heat through gently until the cheese has just melted.

Ladle the soup into warmed bowls, scatter over the croûtons, garnish with fresh sage sprigs and serve immediately.

SERVES 6

25 g/1 oz butter
2 shallots, finely chopped
225 g/8 oz potatoes, diced
4 tbsp plain flour
2 tbsp dry white wine
300 ml/10 fl oz milk
325 g/11½ oz canned sweetcorn, drained
85 g/3 oz Gruyère, Emmenthal or Cheddar cheese, grated
8–10 fresh sage leaves, chopped
425 ml/15 fl oz double cream
fresh sage sprigs, to garnish

croûtons

2–3 slices of day-old white bread
2 tbsp olive oil

Cheese & Bacon Soup

Melt the butter in a large saucepan over a medium heat. Add the garlic and onion and cook, stirring, for 3 minutes, until slightly softened. Add the chopped bacon and leeks and cook for a further 3 minutes, stirring.

In a bowl, mix the flour with enough stock to make a smooth paste, then stir it into the pan. Cook, stirring, for 2 minutes. Pour in the remaining stock, then add the potatoes. Season with salt and pepper. Bring the soup to the boil, then lower the heat and simmer gently for 25 minutes, until the potatoes are tender and cooked through.

Stir in the cream and cook for 5 minutes, then gradually stir in the cheese until melted. Remove from the heat and ladle into serving bowls. Garnish with grated Cheddar cheese and serve immediately.

SERVES 4

2 tbsp butter

2 garlic cloves, chopped

1 large onion, sliced

250 g/9 oz smoked lean back bacon, chopped

2 large leeks, trimmed and sliced

2 tbsp plain flour

1 litre/$1^3/4$ pints vegetable stock

450 g/1 lb potatoes, chopped

100 ml/$3^1/2$ fl oz double cream

300 g/$10^1/2$ oz grated Cheddar cheese, plus extra to garnish

salt and pepper

Sausage & Red Cabbage Soup

Heat the oil in a large saucepan. Add the garlic and onion and cook over a medium heat, stirring, for 3 minutes, until slightly softened. Add the leek and cook for a further 3 minutes, stirring.

In a bowl, mix the cornflour with enough stock to make a smooth paste, then stir it into the pan. Cook, stirring, for 2 minutes. Stir in the remaining stock, then add the potatoes and sausages. Season with salt and pepper. Bring to the boil, then lower the heat and simmer for 25 minutes.

Add the red cabbage and beans and cook for 10 minutes, then stir in the cream and cook for a further 5 minutes. Remove from the heat and ladle into serving bowls. Garnish with ground paprika and serve immediately.

SERVES 4

2 tbsp olive oil

1 garlic clove, chopped

1 large onion, chopped

1 large leek, sliced

2 tbsp cornflour

1 litre/$1^3/_4$ pints vegetable stock

450 g/1 lb potatoes, sliced

200 g/7 oz skinless sausages, sliced

150 g/$5^1/_2$ oz red cabbage, chopped

200 g/7 oz canned black-eye
    beans, drained

125 ml/4 fl oz double cream

salt and pepper

ground paprika, to garnish

Spicy Lamb Soup with Chickpeas & Courgettes

Heat 1 tablespoon of the oil in a large saucepan or cast-iron casserole over a medium-high heat. Add the lamb, in batches if necessary to avoid crowding the pan, and cook until evenly browned on all sides, adding a little more oil if needed. Remove the meat with a slotted spoon when browned.

Reduce the heat and add the onion and garlic to the pan. Cook, stirring frequently, for 1–2 minutes.

Add the water and return all the meat to the pan. Bring just to the boil and skim off any scum that rises to the surface. Reduce the heat and stir in the tomatoes, bay leaf, thyme, oregano, cinnamon, cumin, turmeric and harissa. Simmer for about 1 hour, or until the meat is very tender. Discard the bay leaf.

Stir in the chickpeas, carrot and potato and simmer for 15 minutes. Add the courgette and peas and continue simmering for 15–20 minutes, or until all the vegetables are tender.

Taste and add more harissa, if desired. Ladle the soup into warmed bowls and garnish with mint or coriander.

SERVES 4–6

1–2 tbsp olive oil

450 g/1 lb lean boneless lamb, such as shoulder or neck fillet, trimmed of fat and cut into 1-cm/^{1}/$_2$-inch cubes

1 onion, finely chopped

2–3 garlic cloves, crushed

1.2 litres/2 pints water

400 g/14 oz canned chopped tomatoes

1 bay leaf

^{1}/$_2$ tsp dried thyme

^{1}/$_2$ tsp dried oregano

^{1}/$_8$ tsp ground cinnamon

^{1}/$_4$ tsp ground cumin

^{1}/$_4$ tsp ground turmeric

1 tsp harissa, or more to taste

400 g/14 oz canned chickpeas, rinsed and drained

1 carrot, diced

1 potato, diced

1 courgette, quartered lengthways and sliced

100 g/3^1/$_2$ oz fresh or defrosted frozen green peas

sprigs of fresh mint or coriander, to garnish

Scotch Broth

Heat the vegetable oil in a large, heavy-based saucepan and add the pieces of lamb, turning them to seal and brown on both sides. Lift the lamb out of the pan and set aside until required.

Add the onion, carrots and leeks to the saucepan and cook gently for about 3 minutes.

Return the lamb to the saucepan and add the vegetable stock, bay leaf, parsley and pearl barley to the saucepan. Bring the mixture in the pan to the boil, then reduce the heat. Cover and simmer for 1½ –2 hours.

Discard the parsley sprigs. Lift the pieces of lamb from the broth and allow them to cool slightly. Remove the bones and any fat and chop the meat. Return the lamb to the broth and reheat gently. Season to taste with salt and pepper.

It is advisable to prepare this soup a day ahead, then leave it to cool, cover and refrigerate overnight. When ready to serve, remove and discard the layer of fat from the surface and reheat the soup gently. Ladle into warmed bowls and serve immediately.

SERVES 4

1 tbsp vegetable oil

500 g/1 lb 2 oz lean neck of lamb

1 large onion, sliced

2 carrots, sliced

2 leeks, sliced

1 litre/1¾ pints vegetable stock

1 bay leaf

sprigs of fresh parsley

55 g/2 oz pearl barley

salt and pepper

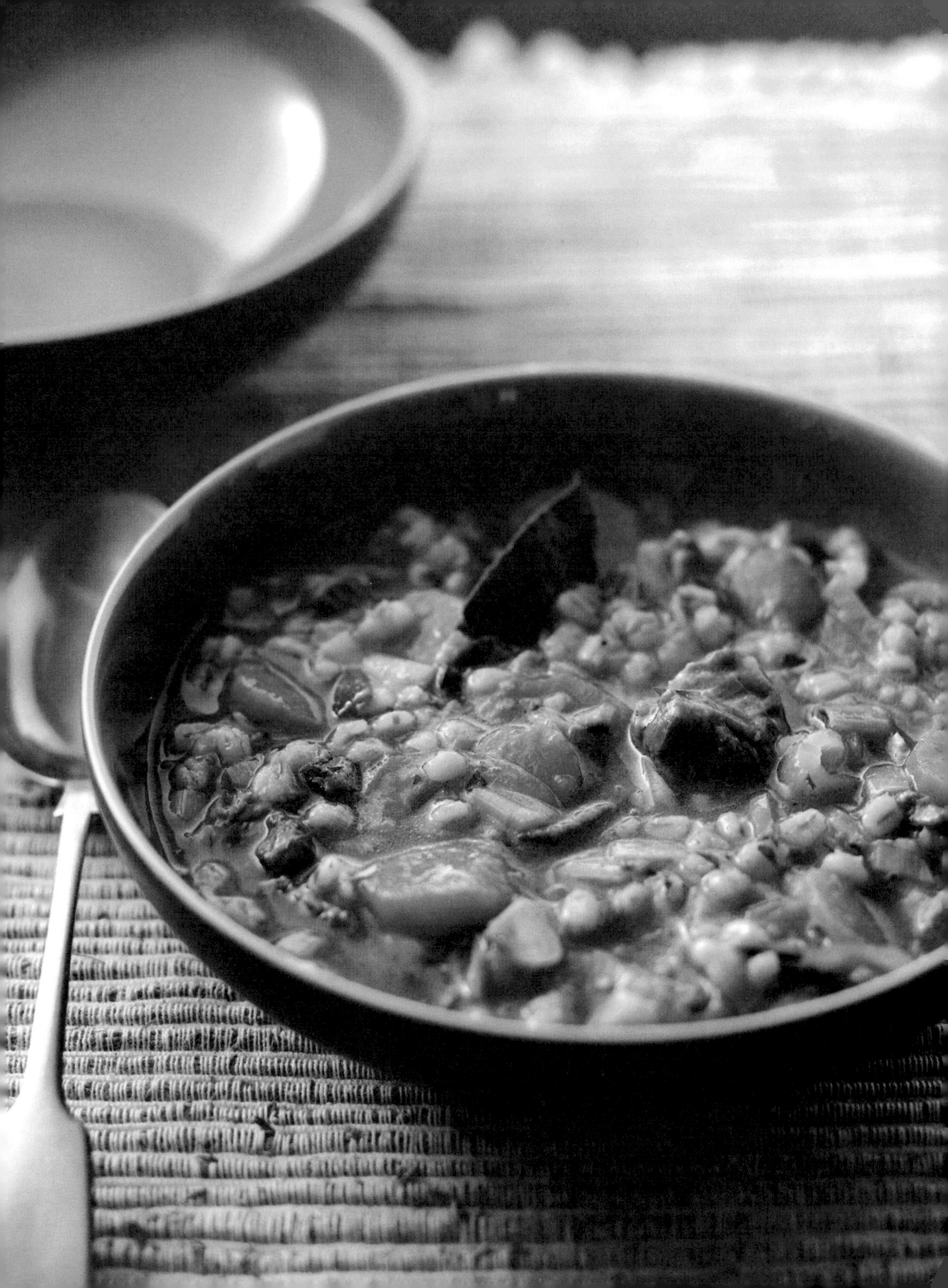

Beef & Bean Soup

Heat the oil in a large saucepan over a medium heat. Add the onion and garlic and cook, stirring frequently, for 5 minutes, or until softened. Add the pepper and carrots and cook for a further 5 minutes.

Meanwhile, drain the beans, reserving the liquid from the can. Place two thirds of the beans, reserving the remainder, in a food processor or blender with the bean liquid and process until smooth.

Add the beef to the saucepan and cook, stirring constantly, to break up any lumps, until well browned. Add the spices and cook, stirring, for 2 minutes. Add the cabbage, tomatoes, stock and puréed beans and season to taste with salt and pepper. Bring to the boil, then reduce the heat, cover and simmer for 15 minutes, or until the vegetables are tender.

Stir in the reserved beans, cover and simmer for a further 5 minutes. Ladle the soup into warmed soup bowls and serve.

SERVES 4

2 tbsp vegetable oil

1 large onion, finely chopped

2 garlic cloves, finely chopped

1 green pepper, deseeded and sliced

2 carrots, sliced

400 g/14 oz canned black-eye beans

225 g/8 oz fresh beef mince

1 tsp each ground cumin, chilli
   powder and paprika

$^{1}/_{4}$ cabbage, sliced

225 g/8 oz tomatoes, peeled and
   chopped

600 ml/1 pint beef stock

salt and pepper

Chicken & Potato Soup with Bacon

Melt the butter in a large saucepan over a medium heat. Add the garlic and onion and cook, stirring, for 3 minutes, until slightly softened. Add the chopped bacon and leeks and cook for a further 3 minutes, stirring.

In a bowl, mix the flour with enough stock to make a smooth paste, then stir it into the pan. Cook, stirring, for 2 minutes. Pour in the remaining stock, then add the potatoes and chicken. Season with salt and pepper. Bring to the boil, then lower the heat and simmer for 25 minutes, until the chicken and potatoes are tender and cooked through.

Stir in the cream and cook for a further 2 minutes, then remove from the heat and ladle into serving bowls. Garnish with the grilled bacon and flat-leaf parsley, and serve immediately.

SERVES 4

1 tbsp butter

2 garlic cloves, chopped

1 onion, sliced

250 g/9 oz smoked lean back bacon, chopped

2 large leeks, sliced

2 tbsp plain flour

1 litre/$1^3/_4$ pints chicken stock

800 g/1 lb 12 oz potatoes, chopped

200 g/7 oz skinless chicken breast, chopped

4 tbsp double cream

salt and pepper

grilled bacon and sprigs of fresh flat-leaf parsley, to garnish

Chicken Gumbo Soup

Heat the oil in a large heavy-based saucepan over a medium-low heat and stir in the flour. Cook for about 15 minutes, stirring occasionally, until the mixture is a rich golden brown.

Add the onion, green pepper and celery and continue cooking for about 10 minutes until the onion softens.

Slowly pour in the stock and bring to the boil, stirring well and scraping the bottom of the pan to mix in the flour. Remove the pan from the heat.

Add the tomatoes and garlic. Stir in the okra and rice and season to taste with salt and pepper. Reduce the heat, cover and simmer for 20 minutes, or until the okra is tender.

Add the chicken and sausage and continue simmering for about 10 minutes. Taste and adjust the seasoning, if necessary, and ladle into warmed bowls to serve.

SERVES 6

2 tbsp olive oil

4 tbsp plain flour

1 onion, finely chopped

1 small green pepper, deseeded and finely chopped

1 celery stick, finely chopped

1.2 litres/2 pints chicken stock

400 g/14 oz canned chopped tomatoes

3 garlic cloves, finely chopped or crushed

125 g/4$\frac{1}{2}$ oz okra, stems removed, cut into 5-mm/$\frac{1}{4}$-inch thick slices

50 g/1$\frac{3}{4}$ oz white rice

200 g/7 oz cooked chicken, cubed

115 g/4 oz cooked garlic sausage, sliced or cubed

salt and pepper

Turkey & Lentil Soup

Heat the oil in a large saucepan. Add the garlic and onion and cook over a medium heat, stirring, for 3 minutes, until slightly softened. Add the mushrooms, red pepper and tomatoes and cook for a further 5 minutes, stirring. Pour in the stock and red wine, then add the cauliflower, carrot and red lentils. Season to taste with salt and pepper. Bring to the boil, then lower the heat and simmer the soup gently for 25 minutes, until the vegetables are tender and cooked through.

Add the turkey and courgette to the pan and cook for 10 minutes. Stir in the shredded basil and cook for a further 5 minutes, then remove from the heat and ladle into serving bowls. Garnish with basil and serve immediately.

SERVES 4

1 tbsp olive oil

1 garlic clove, chopped

1 large onion, chopped

200 g/7 oz mushrooms, sliced

1 red pepper, deseeded and
    chopped

6 tomatoes, peeled, deseeded and
    chopped

1.2 litres/2 pints chicken stock

150 ml/5 fl oz red wine

85 g/3 oz cauliflower florets

1 carrot, chopped

200 g/7 oz red lentils

350 g/12 oz cooked turkey,
    chopped

1 courgette, chopped

1 tbsp shredded fresh basil

salt and pepper

sprigs of fresh basil, to garnish

Seafood Chowder

Discard any mussels with broken shells or any that refuse to close when tapped. Rinse, pull off any beards, and if there are barnacles, scrape them off with a knife under cold running water. Put the mussels in a large heavy-based saucepan. Cover tightly and cook over a high heat for about 4 minutes, or until the mussels open, shaking the pan occasionally. Discard any that remain closed. When they are cool enough to handle, remove the mussels from the shells, adding any additional juices to the cooking liquid. Strain the cooking liquid through a muslin-lined sieve and reserve.

Put the flour in a mixing bowl and very slowly whisk in enough of the stock to make a thick paste. Whisk in a little more stock to make a smooth liquid.

Melt the butter in heavy-based saucepan over a medium-low heat. Add the onion, cover and cook for about 5 minutes, stirring frequently, until it softens.

Add the remaining fish stock and bring to the boil. Slowly whisk in the flour mixture until well combined and bring back to the boil, whisking constantly. Add the mussel cooking liquid. Season with salt, if needed, and pepper. Reduce the heat and simmer, partially covered, for 15 minutes.

Add the fish and mussels and continue simmering, stirring occasionally, for about 5 minutes, or until the fish is cooked and begins to flake.

Stir in the prawns and cream. Taste and adjust the seasoning. Simmer for a few minutes longer to heat through. Ladle into warmed bowls, sprinkle with dill and serve.

SERVES 6

1 kg/2 lb 4 oz live mussels

4 tbsp plain flour

1.5 litres/$2^3/_4$ pints fish stock

1 tbsp butter

1 large onion, finely chopped

350 g/12 oz skinless white fish fillets, such as cod, sole or haddock

200 g/7 oz cooked or raw peeled prawns

300 ml/10 fl oz whipping cream or double cream

salt and pepper

snipped fresh dill, to garnish

Breton Fish Soup with Cider & Sorrel

Melt the butter in a large saucepan over a medium-low heat. Add the leek and shallots and cook for about 5 minutes, stirring frequently, until they start to soften. Add the cider and bring to the boil.

Stir in the stock, potatoes and bay leaf with a large pinch of salt (unless the stock is salty) and bring back to the boil. Reduce the heat, cover and cook gently for 10 minutes.

Put the flour in a small bowl and very slowly whisk in a few tablespoons of the milk to make a thick paste. Stir in a little more to make a smooth liquid.

Adjust the heat so the soup bubbles gently. Stir in the flour mixture and cook, stirring frequently, for 5 minutes. Add the remaining milk and half the cream. Continue cooking for about 10 minutes until the potatoes are tender.

Chop the sorrel finely and combine with the remaining cream. (If using a food processor, add the sorrel and chop, then add the cream and process briefly.)

Stir the sorrel cream into the soup and add the fish. Continue cooking, stirring occasionally, for about 3 minutes, until the monkfish stiffens or the cod just begins to flake. Taste the soup and adjust the seasoning, if needed. Ladle into warmed bowls and serve.

SERVES 4

2 tsp butter

1 large leek, thinly sliced

2 shallots, finely chopped

125 ml/4 fl oz dry cider

300 ml/10 fl oz fish stock

250 g/9 oz potatoes, diced

1 bay leaf

4 tbsp plain flour

200 ml/7 fl oz milk

200 ml/7 fl oz double cream

55 g/2 oz fresh sorrel leaves

350 g/12 oz skinless monkfish or cod fillet, cut into 2.5-cm/1-inch pieces

salt and pepper

Spicy Soups

This chapter explores the world of spice with an exciting selection of internationally-inspired dishes. The recipes range in heat from the warming Beef Goulash Soup to the carefully balanced Hot & Sour Soup with Tofu, and from the fiery Middle Eastern Soup with Harissa to the delicately spiced Thai Chicken-Coconut Soup. All are guaranteed to spice up and add excitement to your mealtimes.

Hot & Sour Soup with Tofu

Put the lime rind, garlic and ginger into a large saucepan with the stock and bring to the boil. Reduce the heat and simmer for 5 minutes. Remove the lime rind, garlic and ginger with a slotted spoon and discard.

Meanwhile, heat the vegetable oil in a large frying pan over a high heat, add the tofu and cook, turning frequently, until golden. Remove from the pan and drain on kitchen paper.

Add the noodles, mushrooms and chilli to the stock and simmer for 3 minutes. Add the tofu, spring onions, soy sauce, lime juice, rice wine and sesame oil and briefly heat through.

Divide the soup among 4 warmed bowls, scatter over the coriander and serve immediately.

SERVES 4

3 strips of rind and juice of 1 lime

2 garlic cloves, peeled

2 slices fresh root ginger

1 litre/1^3/$_4$ pints chicken stock

1 tbsp vegetable oil

150 g/5^1/$_2$ oz firm tofu (drained weight), cubed

200 g/7 oz dried fine egg noodles

100 g/3^1/$_2$ oz shiitake mushrooms, sliced

1 fresh red chilli, deseeded and sliced

4 spring onions, sliced

1 tsp soy sauce

1 tsp Chinese rice wine

1 tsp sesame oil

chopped fresh coriander, to garnish

Mushroom & Ginger Soup

Soak the dried Chinese mushrooms (if using) for at least 30 minutes in 300 ml/10 fl oz of the hot stock. Drain the mushrooms and reserve the stock. Remove the stalks of the mushrooms and discard. Slice the caps and reserve. Cook the noodles for 2–3 minutes in boiling water, then drain and rinse. Reserve until required.

Heat the sunflower oil in a preheated wok or large, heavy-based frying pan over a high heat. Add the garlic and ginger, stir and add the mushrooms. Stir over a high heat for 2 minutes.

Add the remaining vegetable stock with the reserved stock and bring to the boil. Add the mushroom ketchup and soy sauce. Stir in the beansprouts and cook until tender.

Place some noodles in each soup bowl and ladle the soup on top. Garnish with fresh coriander sprigs and serve immediately.

SERVES 4

15 g/^{1}/$_2$ oz dried Chinese mushrooms or 125 g/4^1/$_2$ oz field or chestnut mushrooms

1 litre/1^3/$_4$ pints hot vegetable stock

125 g/4^1/$_2$ oz thread egg noodles

2 tsp sunflower oil

3 garlic cloves, crushed

2.5-cm/1-inch piece fresh root ginger, finely shredded

^{1}/$_2$ tsp mushroom ketchup

1 tsp light soy sauce

125 g/4^1/$_2$ oz beansprouts

fresh coriander sprigs, to garnish

Curried Courgette Soup

Melt the butter in a large saucepan over a medium heat. Add the onion and cook for about 3 minutes until it begins to soften.

Add the courgettes, stock and curry powder, along with a large pinch of salt, if using unsalted stock. Bring the soup to the boil, reduce the heat, cover and cook gently for about 25 minutes until the vegetables are tender.

Allow the soup to cool slightly, then transfer to a food processor or blender, working in batches if necessary. Process the soup until just smooth, but still with green flecks. (If using a food processor, strain off the cooking liquid and reserve. Process the soup solids with enough cooking liquid to moisten them, then combine with the remaining liquid.)

Return the soup to the rinsed-out saucepan and stir in the soured cream. Reheat gently over a low heat just until hot. (Do not boil.)

Taste and adjust the seasoning, if needed. Ladle into warmed bowls, garnish with a swirl of soured cream and serve.

SERVES 4

2 tsp butter

1 large onion, finely chopped

900 g/2 lb courgettes, sliced

450 ml/16 fl oz chicken or vegetable stock

1 tsp curry powder

125 ml/4 fl oz soured cream, plus extra to garnish

salt and pepper

Mulligatawny Soup

Melt the butter in a large saucepan over a medium heat, add the onions and sauté gently until soft but not brown.

Add the turnip, carrots and apple and continue to cook for a further 3–4 minutes.

Stir in the curry powder until the vegetables are well coated, then pour in the stock. Bring to the boil, cover and simmer for about 45 minutes. Season well with salt and pepper to taste and add the lemon juice.

Transfer the soup to a food processor or blender. Process until smooth and return to the rinsed-out saucepan. Add the chicken and coriander to the saucepan and heat through.

Place a spoonful of rice in each serving bowl and pour the soup over the top. Garnish with coriander and serve.

SERVES 4–6

55 g/2 oz butter

2 onions, chopped

1 small turnip, cut into small dice

2 carrots, finely sliced

1 Cox's apple, cored, peeled and chopped

2 tbsp mild curry powder

1.2 litres/2 pints chicken stock

juice of $^1/_2$ lemon

175 g/6 oz cold cooked chicken, cut into small pieces

2 tbsp chopped fresh coriander, plus extra to garnish

salt and pepper

55 g/2 oz cooked rice, to serve

Thai Chicken-Coconut Soup

Soak the dried noodles in a large bowl with enough lukewarm water to cover for 20 minutes, until soft. Alternatively, cook according to the packet instructions. Drain well and set aside.

Meanwhile, bring the stock to the boil in a large saucepan over a high heat. Lower the heat, add the lemon grass, ginger, lime leaves and chilli and simmer for 5 minutes. Add the chicken and continue simmering for a further 3 minutes, or until cooked. Stir in the coconut cream, nam pla and lime juice and continue simmering for 3 minutes. Add the beansprouts and spring onions and simmer for a further 1 minute. Taste and gradually add extra nam pla or lime juice at this point, if needed. Remove and discard the lemon grass stalk.

Divide the vermicelli noodles between 4 bowls. Bring the soup back to the boil, then add the soup to each bowl. The heat of the soup will warm the noodles. To garnish, sprinkle with coriander leaves.

SERVES 4

115 g/4 oz dried cellophane noodles

1.2 litres/2 pints chicken or vegetable stock

1 lemon grass stalk, crushed

1-cm/^{1}/$_2$-inch piece fresh root ginger, peeled and very finely chopped

2 fresh kaffir lime leaves, thinly sliced

1 fresh red chilli, or to taste, deseeded and thinly sliced

2 skinless, boneless chicken breasts, thinly sliced

200 ml/7 fl oz coconut cream

2 tbsp nam pla (Thai fish sauce)

1 tbsp fresh lime juice

55 g/2 oz beansprouts

4 spring onions, green part only, finely sliced

fresh coriander leaves, to garnish

Duck with Spring Onion Soup

Slash the skin of the duck 3 or 4 times with a sharp knife and rub in the curry paste. Cook the duck breasts, skin-side down, in a wok or frying pan over a high heat for 2–3 minutes. Turn over, reduce the heat and cook for a further 3–4 minutes, until cooked through. Lift out and slice thickly. Set aside and keep warm.

Meanwhile, heat the oil in a wok or large frying pan and stir-fry half the spring onions, the garlic, ginger, carrots and red pepper for 2–3 minutes. Pour in the stock and add the chilli sauce, soy sauce and mushrooms. Bring to the boil, lower the heat and simmer for 4–5 minutes.

Ladle the soup into warmed bowls, top with the duck slices and garnish with the remaining spring onions. Serve immediately.

SERVES 4

2 duck breasts, skin on

2 tbsp red curry paste

2 tbsp vegetable or groundnut oil

bunch of spring onions, chopped

2 garlic cloves, crushed

5-cm/2-inch piece fresh root ginger, grated

2 carrots, thinly sliced

1 red pepper, deseeded and cut into strips

1 litre/1^1/$_4$ pints chicken stock

2 tbsp sweet chilli sauce

3–4 tbsp Thai soy sauce

400 g/14 oz canned straw mushrooms, drained

Spicy Beef & Noodle Soup

Pour the stock into a large saucepan and bring to the boil. Meanwhile, heat the oil in a wok or large frying pan. Add a third of the noodles and fry for 10–20 seconds, until they have puffed up. Lift out with tongs, drain on kitchen paper and set aside. Discard all but 2 tablespoons of the oil.

Add the shallots, garlic and ginger to the wok or frying pan and stir-fry for 1 minute. Add the beef and curry paste and stir-fry for a further 3–4 minutes, until tender.

Add the beef mixture, the uncooked noodles, soy sauce and fish sauce to the saucepan of stock and simmer for 2–3 minutes, until the noodles have swelled. Serve hot, garnished with the chopped coriander and the reserved crispy noodles.

SERVES 4

1 litre/1³/₄ pints beef stock

150 ml/5 fl oz vegetable or groundnut oil

85 g/3 oz rice vermicelli noodles

2 shallots, thinly sliced

2 garlic cloves, crushed

2.5-cm/1-inch piece fresh root ginger, thinly sliced

225-g/8-oz piece fillet steak, cut into thin strips

2 tbsp green curry paste

2 tbsp Thai soy sauce

1 tbsp fish sauce

chopped fresh coriander, to garnish

Mexican-Style Beef & Rice Soup

Heat half the oil in a large frying pan over a medium-high heat. Add the meat in one layer and cook until well browned, turning to colour all sides. Remove the pan from the heat and pour in the wine.

Heat the remaining oil in a large saucepan over a medium heat. Add the onion, cover and cook for about 3 minutes, stirring occasionally, until just softened. Add the green pepper, chilli, garlic and carrot, and continue cooking, covered, for 3 minutes.

Add the coriander, cumin, cinnamon, oregano, bay leaf and orange rind. Stir in the tomatoes and stock, along with the beef and wine. Bring almost to the boil and when the mixture begins to bubble, reduce the heat to low. Cover and simmer gently, stirring occasionally, for about 1 hour until the meat is tender.

Stir in the rice, raisins and chocolate, and continue cooking, stirring occasionally, for about 30 minutes until the rice is tender.

Ladle into warmed bowls and garnish with coriander.

SERVES 4

3 tbsp olive oil

500 g/1 lb 2 oz boneless stewing beef, cut into 2.5-cm/1-inch pieces

150 ml/5 fl oz red wine

1 onion, finely chopped

1 green pepper, deseeded and finely chopped

1 small fresh red chilli, deseeded and finely chopped

2 garlic cloves, finely chopped

1 carrot, finely chopped

$1/4$ tsp ground coriander

$1/4$ tsp ground cumin

$1/8$ tsp ground cinnamon

$1/4$ tsp dried oregano

1 bay leaf

grated rind of $1/2$ orange

400 g/14 oz canned chopped tomatoes

1.2 litres/2 pints beef stock

50 g/$1^3/4$ oz long-grain white rice

25 g/1 oz raisins

15 g/$1/2$ oz plain chocolate, melted

chopped fresh coriander, to garnish

Beef Goulash Soup

Heat the oil in a large wide saucepan over a medium-high heat. Add the beef and sprinkle with salt and pepper. Fry until lightly browned.

Reduce the heat and add the onions and garlic. Cook for about 3 minutes, stirring frequently, until the onions are softened. Stir in the flour and continue cooking for 1 minute.

Add the water and stir to combine well, scraping the bottom of the pan to mix in the flour. Stir in the tomatoes, carrot, pepper, paprika, caraway seeds, oregano and stock.

Bring just to the boil. Reduce the heat, cover and simmer gently for about 40 minutes, stirring occasionally, until all the vegetables are tender.

Add the tagliatelle to the soup and simmer for a further 20 minutes, or until the tagliatelle is cooked.

Taste the soup and adjust the seasoning, if necessary. Ladle into warmed bowls and top each with a tablespoonful of soured cream. Garnish with coriander and serve.

SERVES 6

1 tbsp oil

500 g/1 lb 2 oz fresh lean beef mince

2 onions, finely chopped

2 garlic cloves, finely chopped

2 tbsp plain flour

225 ml/8 fl oz water

400 g/14 oz canned chopped tomatoes

1 carrot, finely chopped

225 g/8 oz red pepper, roasted, peeled, deseeded and chopped

1 tsp Hungarian paprika

$1/4$ tsp caraway seeds

pinch of dried oregano

1 litre/$1^3/4$ pints beef stock

55 g/2 oz tagliatelle, broken into small pieces

salt and pepper

soured cream and sprigs of fresh coriander, to garnish

Middle Eastern Soup with Harissa

Preheat the oven to 200°C/400°F/Gas Mark 6. Prick the aubergines, place on a baking sheet and bake for 1 hour. When cool, peel and chop.

Heat the oil in a saucepan. Add the lamb and cook until browned. Add the onion, stock and water. Bring to the boil. Reduce the heat and simmer for 1 hour.

For the harissa, process the peppers, coriander seeds, chillies, garlic and caraway seeds in a food processor. With the motor running, add enough oil to make a paste. Add salt to taste, then spoon into a jar. Cover with oil, seal and chill.

Remove the shanks from the stock, cut off the meat and chop. Add the sweet potato, cinnamon and cumin to the stock, bring to the boil, cover and simmer for 20 minutes. Discard the cinnamon and process the mixture in a food processor with the aubergine. Return to the saucepan, add the lamb and coriander and heat until hot. Serve with the harissa.

SERVES 4

2 aubergines

3 tbsp olive oil

6 lamb shanks

1 small onion, chopped

400 ml/14 fl oz chicken stock

2 litres/$3^1/_2$ pints water

400 g/14 oz sweet potato, cut into chunks

5-cm/2-inch piece cinnamon stick

1 tsp ground cumin

2 tbsp chopped fresh coriander

harissa

2 red peppers, roasted, peeled, deseeded and chopped

$^1/_2$ tsp coriander seeds, dry-fried

25 g/1 oz fresh red chillies, chopped

2 garlic cloves, chopped

2 tsp caraway seeds

olive oil

salt

Asian Lamb Soup

Trim all visible fat from the lamb and slice the meat thinly. Cut the slices into bite-sized pieces. Spread the meat in one layer on a plate and sprinkle over the garlic and 1 tablespoon of the soy sauce. Leave to marinate, covered, for at least 10 minutes or up to 1 hour.

Put the stock in a saucepan with the ginger, lemon grass, remaining soy sauce and the chilli purée. Bring just to the boil, reduce the heat, cover and simmer for 10–15 minutes.

When ready to serve the soup, drop the tomatoes, spring onions, beansprouts and fresh coriander leaves into the simmering stock.

Heat the oil in a frying pan and add the lamb with its marinade. Stir-fry the lamb just until it is no longer red and divide among warmed bowls.

Ladle over the hot stock and serve immediately.

SERVES 4

150 g/5^1/$_2$ oz lean tender lamb, such as neck fillet or leg steak

2 garlic cloves, very finely chopped

2 tbsp soy sauce

1.2 litres/2 pints chicken stock

1 tbsp grated fresh root ginger

5-cm/2-inch piece lemon grass, sliced into very thin rounds

^{1}/$_4$ tsp chilli purée, or to taste

6–8 cherry tomatoes, quartered

4 spring onions, sliced finely

50 g/1^3/$_4$ oz beansprouts, snapped in half

2 tbsp fresh coriander leaves

1 tsp olive oil

Wonton Soup

For the wonton filling, mix together the pork, prawns, ginger, soy sauce, rice wine, spring onion, sugar, pepper and sesame oil, and stir well until the texture is thick and pasty. Set aside for at least 20 minutes.

To make the wontons, place a teaspoon of the filling at the centre of a wrapper. Brush the edges with a little egg white. Bring the opposite points towards each other and press the edges together, creating a flower-like shape. Repeat with the remaining wrappers and filling.

To make the soup, bring the stock to the boil and add the salt and pepper. Boil the wontons in the stock for about 5 minutes until the wrappers begin to wrinkle around the filling.

To serve, put the spring onion in individual bowls, spoon in the wontons and soup and top with the coriander.

SERVES 6–8

2 litres/$3^1/_2$ pints chicken stock

2 tsp salt

$^1/_2$ tsp white pepper

2 tbsp finely chopped spring onion, to serve

1 tbsp chopped fresh coriander leaves, to serve

wontons

175 g/6 oz minced pork, not too lean

225 g/8 oz raw prawns, peeled, deveined and chopped

$^1/_2$ tsp finely chopped fresh root ginger

1 tbsp light soy sauce

1 tbsp Shaoxing rice wine

2 tsp finely chopped spring onion

pinch of sugar

pinch of white pepper

dash of sesame oil

30 square wonton wrappers

1 egg white, lightly beaten

Pork & Vegetable Broth

Heat the oil in a large saucepan. Add the garlic and spring onions and cook over a medium heat, stirring, for 3 minutes, until slightly softened. Add the red pepper and cook for a further 5 minutes, stirring.

In a bowl, mix the cornflour with enough of the stock to make a smooth paste, then stir it into the pan. Cook, stirring, for 2 minutes. Stir in the remaining stock and the soy sauce and rice wine, then add the pork, lemon grass, chilli and ginger. Season with salt and pepper. Bring to the boil, then lower the heat and simmer for 25 minutes.

Bring a separate saucepan of water to the boil, add the noodles and cook for 3 minutes. Remove from the heat, drain, then add the noodles to the soup along with the water chestnuts. Cook for a further 2 minutes, then remove from the heat and ladle into serving bowls.

SERVES 4

1 tbsp chilli oil

1 garlic clove, chopped

3 spring onions, sliced

1 red pepper, deseeded and finely sliced

2 tbsp cornflour

1 litre/$1^3/4$ pints vegetable stock

1 tbsp soy sauce

2 tbsp rice wine or dry sherry

150 g/$5^1/2$ oz pork fillet, sliced

1 tbsp finely chopped lemon grass

1 small red chilli, deseeded and finely chopped

1 tbsp grated fresh root ginger

115 g/4 oz fine egg noodles

200 g/7 oz canned water chestnuts, drained and sliced

salt and pepper

Pork Chilli Soup

Heat the oil in a large saucepan over a medium-high heat. Add the pork, season with salt and pepper, and cook until no longer pink, stirring frequently. Reduce the heat to medium and add the onion, celery, red pepper and garlic. Cover and continue cooking for 5 minutes, stirring occasionally, until the onion is softened.

Add the tomato purée, tomatoes and the stock. Add the coriander, cumin, oregano and chilli powder. Stir the ingredients in to combine well.

Bring just to the boil, reduce the heat to low, cover and simmer for 30–40 minutes until all the vegetables are very tender. Taste and adjust the seasoning, adding more chilli powder if you like it hotter.

Ladle the chilli into warmed bowls and sprinkle with coriander. Top each serving with a spoonful of soured cream and serve.

SERVES 4

2 tsp olive oil

500 g/1 lb 2 oz fresh lean pork mince

1 onion, finely chopped

1 celery stick, finely chopped

1 red pepper, cored, deseeded and finely chopped

2–3 garlic cloves, finely chopped

3 tbsp tomato purée

400 g/14 oz canned chopped tomatoes

450 ml/16 fl oz chicken or meat stock

$^1/_8$ tsp ground coriander

$^1/_8$ tsp ground cumin

$^1/_4$ tsp dried oregano

1 tsp mild chilli powder, or to taste

salt and pepper

fresh coriander leaves, to garnish

soured cream, to serve

Sweetcorn & Smoked Chilli Soup

Heat the oil in a large, heavy-based saucepan. Add the onions and cook over a low heat, stirring occasionally, for 5 minutes, or until softened. Stir in the sweetcorn, cover and cook for a further 3 minutes.

Add the stock, half the milk, the chillies and garlic and season with salt. Bring to the boil, reduce the heat, then cover and simmer for 15–20 minutes.

Stir in the remaining milk. Reserve about 175 ml/6 fl oz of the soup solids, draining off as much liquid as possible. Transfer the remaining soup to a food processor or blender and process to a coarse purée.

Return the soup to the saucepan and stir in the reserved soup solids, the chorizo, lime juice and coriander. Reheat to simmering point, stirring constantly. Ladle into warmed bowls and serve immediately.

SERVES 4

1 tbsp sunflower oil

2 onions, chopped

550 g/1 lb 4 oz frozen sweetcorn kernels, thawed

600 ml/1 pint chicken stock

425 ml/15 fl oz milk

4 chipotle chillies, deseeded and finely chopped

2 garlic cloves, finely chopped

55 g/2 oz chorizo sausage, thinly sliced

2 tbsp lime juice

2 tbsp chopped fresh coriander

salt

Prawn Laksa

Buy unpeeled prawns, ideally with heads still intact, because you can add the shells and heads to the simmering stock to intensify the flavour.

Peel and devein the prawns. Put the fish stock, salt and the prawn heads, peels and tails in a saucepan over a high heat and slowly bring to the boil. Lower the heat and simmer for 10 minutes.

Meanwhile, make the laksa paste. Put all the ingredients except the oil in a food processor and blend. With the motor running, slowly add up to 2 tablespoons oil just until a paste forms. (If your food processor is too large to work efficiently with this small quantity, use a pestle and mortar, or make double the quantity and keep leftovers tightly covered in the refrigerator to use another time.)

Heat the oil in a large saucepan over a high heat. Add the paste and stir-fry until it is fragrant. Strain the stock through a sieve lined with muslin. Stir the stock into the laksa paste, along with the coconut milk, nam pla and lime juice. Bring to the boil, then lower the heat, cover and simmer for 30 minutes.

Meanwhile, soak the noodles in a large bowl with enough lukewarm water to cover for 20 minutes, until soft. Alternatively, cook according to the packet instructions. Drain and set aside.

Add the prawns and beansprouts to the soup and continue simmering just until the prawns turn opaque and curl. Divide the noodles between 4 bowls and ladle the soup over, making sure everyone gets an equal share of the prawns. Garnish with the coriander and serve.

SERVES 4

20–24 large raw unpeeled prawns
450 ml/16 fl oz fish stock
pinch of salt
1 tsp groundnut oil
450 ml/16 fl oz coconut milk
2 tsp nam pla (Thai fish sauce)
$1/2$ tbsp lime juice
115 g/4 oz dried medium rice
    noodles
55 g/2 oz beansprouts
sprigs of fresh coriander, to garnish

laksa paste

6 coriander stalks with leaves
3 large garlic cloves, crushed
1 fresh red chilli, deseeded and
    chopped
1 lemon grass stalk, centre part
    only, chopped
2.5-cm/1-inch piece fresh root
    ginger, peeled and chopped
$1^1/2$ tbsp shrimp paste
$1/2$ tsp turmeric
2 tbsp groundnut oil

Thai-Style Seafood Soup

Put the stock in a saucepan with the lemon grass, lime rind, ginger and chilli purée. Bring just to the boil, reduce the heat, cover and simmer for 10–15 minutes.

Cut the prawns almost in half lengthways, keeping the tail intact.

Strain the stock, return to the saucepan and bring to a simmer. Add the spring onions and cook for 2–3 minutes. Taste and season with salt, if needed, and stir in a little more chilli purée if wished.

Add the scallops and prawns and poach for about 1 minute until they turn opaque and the prawns curl.

Stir in the fresh coriander leaves, ladle the soup into warmed bowls, dividing the shellfish evenly, and garnish with chillies.

SERVES 4

1.2 litres/2 pints fish stock

1 lemon grass stalk, split lengthways

pared rind of $^1/_2$ lime, or 1 lime leaf

2.5-cm/1-inch piece fresh root
  ginger, sliced

$^1/_4$ tsp chilli purée, or to taste

200 g/7 oz large or medium raw
  prawns, peeled

4–6 spring onions, sliced

250 g/9 oz scallops

2 tbsp fresh coriander leaves

salt

finely chopped red chillies,
  to garnish

Sweetcorn & Crab Soup

Heat the oil in a large frying pan and fry the garlic, shallots, lemon grass and ginger over a low heat, stirring occasionally, for 2–3 minutes, until softened. Add the stock and coconut milk and bring to the boil. Add the sweetcorn, lower the heat and simmer gently for 3–4 minutes.

Add the crabmeat, fish sauce, lime juice and sugar and simmer gently for 1 minute. Ladle into warmed bowls, garnish with the chopped coriander and serve immediately.

SERVES 6

2 tbsp vegetable or groundnut oil

4 garlic cloves, finely chopped

5 shallots, finely chopped

2 lemon grass stalks, finely chopped

2.5-cm/1-inch piece fresh root
 ginger, finely chopped

1 litre/1³/₄ pints chicken stock

400 g/14 oz canned coconut milk

225 g/8 oz frozen sweetcorn
 kernels

350 g/12 oz canned crabmeat,
 drained and shredded

2 tbsp fish sauce

juice of 1 lime

1 tsp palm sugar or soft light brown
 sugar

bunch of fresh coriander, chopped,
 to garnish

Light & Refreshing Soups

The recipes in this section are light in texture and fresh in taste, making them perfect for the summer months or as an elegant starter. Try Chilled Avocado Soup on a hot day, or Parsnip Soup with Ginger & Orange when it's a little cooler. Remember that the fresher the ingredients, the fuller the flavour of the soup – make sure that you use fresh seasonal produce for perfect results.

Golden Vegetable Soup with Green Lentils

Heat the oil in a large saucepan over a medium heat, add the onion, garlic and carrot and cook for 3–4 minutes, stirring frequently, until the onion starts to soften. Add the cabbage and cook for a further 2 minutes.

Add the tomatoes, thyme and 1 bay leaf, then pour in the stock. Bring to the boil, reduce the heat to low and cook gently, partially covered, for about 45 minutes until the vegetables are tender.

Meanwhile, put the lentils in another saucepan with the remaining bay leaf and the water. Bring just to the boil, reduce the heat and simmer for about 25 minutes until tender. Drain off any remaining water, and set aside.

When the vegetable soup is cooked, allow it to cool slightly, then transfer to a food processor or blender and process until smooth, working in batches, if necessary. (If using a food processor, strain off the cooking liquid and reserve. Purée the soup solids with enough cooking liquid to moisten them, then combine with the remaining liquid.)

Return the soup to the saucepan and add the cooked lentils. Taste and adjust the seasoning, and cook for about 10 minutes to heat through. Ladle into warmed bowls and garnish with parsley.

SERVES 6

1 tbsp olive oil

1 onion, finely chopped

1 garlic clove, finely chopped

1 carrot, halved and thinly sliced

450 g/1 lb young green cabbage, cored, quartered and thinly sliced

400 g/14 oz canned chopped tomatoes

$^1/_2$ tsp dried thyme

2 bay leaves

1.5 litres/2$^3/_4$ pints chicken or vegetable stock

200 g/7 oz Puy lentils

450 ml/16 fl oz water

salt and pepper

chopped fresh parsley, to garnish

Sweet & Sour Cabbage Soup

Put the sultanas in a bowl, pour the orange juice over and leave for 15 minutes.

Heat the oil in a large saucepan over a medium heat, add the onion, cover and cook for 3–4 minutes, stirring frequently, until it starts to soften. Add the cabbage and cook for a further 2 minutes; do not allow it to brown.

Add the apples and apple juice, cover and cook gently for 5 minutes.

Stir in the tomatoes, tomato juice, pineapple and water. Season with salt and pepper and add the vinegar. Add the sultanas together with the orange juice soaking liquid. Bring to the boil, reduce the heat and simmer, partially covered, for about 1 hour until the fruit and vegetables are tender.

Allow the soup to cool slightly, then transfer to a food processor or blender and process until smooth, working in batches if necessary. (If using a food processor, strain off the cooking liquid and reserve. Purée the soup solids with enough cooking liquid to moisten them, then combine with the remaining liquid.)

Return the soup to the rinsed-out saucepan and simmer gently for about 10 minutes to reheat. Ladle into warmed bowls. Garnish with mint leaves and serve immediately.

SERVES 4–6

70 g/2^1/$_2$ oz sultanas

125 ml/4 fl oz orange juice

1 tbsp olive oil

1 large onion, chopped

250 g/9 oz shredded cabbage

2 apples, peeled and diced

125 ml/4 fl oz apple juice

400 g/14 oz canned peeled tomatoes

225 ml/8 fl oz tomato or vegetable juice

100 g/3^1/$_2$ oz pineapple flesh, finely chopped

1.2 litres/2 pints water

2 tsp wine vinegar

salt and pepper

fresh mint leaves, to garnish

Parsnip Soup with Ginger & Orange

Heat the olive oil in a large saucepan over a medium heat. Add the onion and leek and cook for about 5 minutes, stirring occasionally, until softened,

Add the carrots, parsnips, ginger, garlic, grated orange rind, water and a large pinch of salt. Reduce the heat, cover and simmer for about 40 minutes, stirring occasionally, until the vegetables are very soft.

Allow the soup to cool slightly, then transfer to a food processor or blender and process until smooth, working in batches if necessary. (If using a food processor, strain off the cooking liquid and reserve. Purée the soup solids with enough cooking liquid to moisten them, then combine with the remaining liquid.)

Return the soup to the rinsed-out saucepan and stir in the orange juice. Add a little water or more orange juice, if you prefer a thinner consistency. Taste and adjust the seasoning if necessary. Simmer for about 10 minutes to heat through.

Ladle into warm bowls, garnish with chives and serve.

SERVES 6

2 tsp olive oil

1 large onion, chopped

1 large leek, sliced

2 carrots, thinly sliced

800 g/1 lb 12 oz parsnips, sliced

4 tbsp grated fresh root ginger

2–3 garlic cloves, finely chopped

grated rind of $^1/_2$ orange

1.4 litres/$2^1/_2$ pints water

225 ml/8 fl oz orange juice

salt and pepper

snipped chives, to garnish

Carrot, Apple & Celery Soup

Place the carrots, onion and celery in a large saucepan and add the vegetable stock. Bring to the boil, reduce the heat, cover and simmer for 10 minutes.

Meanwhile, peel, core and dice 2 of the apples. Add the diced apple, tomato purée, bay leaf and sugar to the saucepan and bring to the boil over a medium heat. Reduce the heat, partially cover and simmer for 20 minutes. Remove and discard the bay leaf.

Meanwhile, wash and core the remaining apple and cut into thin slices, without peeling. Place the apple slices in a small saucepan and squeeze over the lemon juice. Heat the apple slices gently and simmer for 1–2 minutes, or until the apple is tender. Drain the apple slices and reserve until required.

Place the carrot and apple mixture in a food processor or blender and process until smooth. Return the soup to the rinsed-out saucepan, reheat gently, if necessary, and season to taste with salt and pepper. Ladle the soup into 4 warmed bowls, top with the reserved apple slices and shredded celery leaves and serve immediately.

SERVES 4

900 g/2 lb carrots, finely diced

1 medium onion, chopped

3 celery sticks, diced

1 litre/$1^3/_4$ pints vegetable stock

3 medium-sized eating apples

2 tbsp tomato purée

1 bay leaf

2 tsp caster sugar

$1/_4$ large lemon

salt and pepper

shredded celery leaves, to garnish

Beans & Greens Soup

Pick over the beans, cover generously with cold water and leave to soak for 6 hours or overnight. Drain the beans, put in a saucepan and add enough cold water to cover by 5 cm/2 inches. Bring to the boil and boil for 10 minutes. Drain and rinse well.

Heat the oil in a large saucepan over a medium heat. Add the onions and cook, covered, for 3–4 minutes, stirring occasionally, until the onions are just softened. Add the garlic, celery and carrots, and continue cooking for 2 minutes.

Add the water, drained beans, thyme, marjoram and bay leaf. When the mixture begins to bubble, reduce the heat to low. Cover and simmer gently, stirring occasionally, for about 1¼ hours until the beans are tender; the cooking time will vary depending on the type of bean. Season with salt and pepper.

Allow the soup to cool slightly, then transfer 450 ml/16 fl oz to a food processor or blender. Process until smooth and recombine with the soup.

A handful at a time, cut the greens crossways into thin ribbons, keeping tender leaves like spinach separate. Add the thicker leaves and cook gently, uncovered, for 10 minutes. Stir in any remaining greens and continue cooking for 5–10 minutes, until all the greens are tender.

Taste and adjust the seasoning, if necessary. Ladle the soup into warmed bowls and serve.

SERVES 4

250 g/9 oz dried haricot or cannellini beans

1 tbsp olive oil

2 onions, finely chopped

4 garlic cloves, finely chopped

1 celery stick, thinly sliced

2 carrots, halved and thinly sliced

1.2 litres/2 pints water

^{1}/4 tsp dried thyme

^{1}/4 tsp dried marjoram

1 bay leaf

125 g/4^1/2 oz leafy greens, such as chard, mustard, spinach and kale, washed

salt and pepper

Minted Pea & Yogurt Soup

Heat the oil in a saucepan, add the onions and potato and cook over a low heat, stirring occasionally, for about 3 minutes, until the onion is soft and translucent.

Stir in the garlic, ginger, coriander, cumin and flour and cook, stirring constantly, for 1 minute.

Add the stock, peas and the chopped mint and bring to the boil, stirring. Reduce the heat, cover and simmer gently for 15 minutes, or until the vegetables are tender.

Process the soup, in batches, in a food processor or blender. Return the mixture to the pan and season with salt and pepper to taste. Blend the yogurt with the cornflour to a smooth paste and stir into the soup. Add the milk and bring almost to the boil, stirring constantly. Cook very gently for 2 minutes.

Serve the soup hot, garnished with the mint sprigs and a swirl of yogurt.

SERVES 6

2 tbsp vegetable or sunflower oil

2 onions, coarsely chopped

225 g/8 oz potato, coarsely chopped

2 garlic cloves, crushed

2.5-cm/1-inch piece fresh root ginger, chopped

1 tsp ground coriander

1 tsp ground cumin

1 tbsp plain flour

850 ml/1$^1/_2$ pints vegetable stock

500 g/1 lb 2 oz frozen peas

2–3 tbsp chopped fresh mint, plus extra sprigs to garnish

150 ml/5 fl oz pint strained Greek yogurt, plus extra to serve

$^1/_2$ tsp cornflour

300 ml/10 fl oz milk

salt and pepper

Spinach Soup

Heat the oil in a heavy-based saucepan over a medium heat. Add the onion and leek and cook for about 3 minutes, stirring occasionally, until they begin to soften.

Add the potato, water, marjoram, thyme and bay leaf, along with a large pinch of salt. Bring to the boil, reduce the heat, cover and cook gently for about 25 minutes until the vegetables are tender. Remove the bay leaf and the herb stems.

Add the spinach and continue cooking for 3–4 minutes, stirring frequently, just until it is completely wilted.

Allow the soup to cool slightly, then transfer to a food processor or blender and process until smooth, working in batches if necessary. (If using a food processor, strain off the cooking liquid and reserve. Purée the soup solids with enough cooking liquid to moisten them, then combine with the remaining liquid.)

Return the soup to the rinsed-out saucepan and thin with a little more water, if wished. Season with salt, a good grinding of pepper and a generous grating of nutmeg. Place over a low heat and simmer until reheated.

Ladle the soup into warmed bowls and swirl a tablespoonful of cream into each serving.

SERVES 4

1 tbsp olive oil

1 onion, halved and thinly sliced

1 leek, split lengthways and thinly sliced

1 potato, finely diced

1 litre/1^3/$_4$ pints water

2 sprigs fresh marjoram or ^{1}/$_4$ tsp dried

2 sprigs fresh thyme or ^{1}/$_4$ tsp dried

1 bay leaf

400 g/14 oz young spinach, washed

freshly grated nutmeg

salt and pepper

4 tbsp single cream, to serve

Miso Soup

Put the water in a large pan with the dashi granules and bring to the boil. Add the tofu and mushrooms, reduce the heat, and let simmer for 3 minutes.

Stir in the miso paste and let simmer gently, stirring, until it has dissolved.

Add the spring onions and serve immediately. If you leave the soup, the miso will settle, so give the soup a thorough stir before serving to recombine.

SERVES 4

1 litre/$1^3/_4$ pints water

2 tsp dashi granules

175 g/6 oz silken tofu, drained and
   cut into small cubes

4 shiitake mushrooms, finely sliced

4 tbsp miso paste

2 spring onions, chopped

Gazpacho

Tear the bread into pieces and place in a food processor or blender. Process briefly to make breadcrumbs and transfer to a large bowl. Add the tomatoes, garlic, red peppers, cucumber, oil, vinegar and tomato purée. Mix well.

Working in batches, place the tomato mixture with about the same amount of the measured water in the food processor or blender and process to a purée. Transfer to another bowl. When all the tomato mixture and water have been blended together, stir well and season to taste with salt and pepper. Cover with clingfilm and chill in the refrigerator for at least 2 hours, but no longer than 12 hours.

When ready to serve, pour the soup into chilled serving bowls and float an ice cube in each bowl.

SERVES 4

250 g/9 oz white bread slices, crusts removed

700 g/1 lb 9 oz tomatoes, peeled and chopped

3 garlic cloves, coarsely chopped

2 red peppers, deseeded and coarsely chopped

1 cucumber, peeled, deseeded and chopped

5 tbsp extra virgin olive oil

5 tbsp red wine vinegar

1 tbsp tomato purée

850 ml/1^1/$_2$ pints water

salt and pepper

4 ice cubes, to serve

Chilled Avocado Soup

Put the lemon juice into a blender or food processor. Halve the avocados and remove the stones. Scoop out the flesh and chop coarsely.

Place the avocado flesh, chives, parsley, stock, cream and Worcestershire sauce in the blender and process to a smooth purée.

Transfer to a bowl and season to taste with salt and pepper. Cover the bowl tightly with clingfilm and chill in the refrigerator for at least 30 minutes.

To serve, stir, then ladle into chilled soup bowls and garnish with a swirl of cream and a sprinkling of snipped chives.

SERVES 4

1 tbsp lemon juice

2 avocados

1 tbsp snipped fresh chives,
   plus extra to garnish

1 tbsp chopped fresh flat-leaf
   parsley

425 ml/15 fl oz cold chicken stock

300 ml/10 fl oz single cream,
   plus extra to garnish

dash of Worcestershire sauce

salt and pepper

Chilled Borscht

Cover the cabbage generously with cold water in a pan. Bring to the boil, boil for 3 minutes, then drain.

Heat the oil in a large saucepan over a medium-low heat. Add the onion and leek, cover and cook for about 5 minutes, stirring occasionally, until the vegetables begin to soften.

Add the tomatoes, water, carrot, parsnip, beetroot and bay leaf. Stir in the blanched cabbage and add a large pinch of salt. Bring to the boil, reduce the heat and simmer for about 1¼ hours until all the vegetables are tender. Remove and discard the bay leaf.

Allow the soup to cool slightly, then transfer to a food processor or blender and process until smooth, working in batches if necessary. (If using a food processor, strain off the cooking liquid and reserve. Purée the soup solids with enough cooking liquid to moisten them, then combine with the remaining liquid.)

Scrape the soup into a large container and stir in the tomato juice. Allow to cool and refrigerate until cold.

Add the dill and stir. Thin the soup with more tomato juice or water, if wished. Season to taste with salt and pepper and, if you prefer it less sweet, add a few drops of lemon juice. Ladle into chilled soup bowls and top with a spoonful of soured cream and a sprig of dill.

SERVES 4–6

¼ medium cabbage, cored and coarsely chopped

1 tbsp vegetable oil

1 onion, finely chopped

1 leek, halved lengthways and sliced

400 g/14 oz canned peeled tomatoes in juice

1.2 litres/2 pints water, plus extra if needed

1 carrot, thinly sliced

1 small parsnip, finely chopped

3 beetroot (raw or cooked), peeled and cubed

1 bay leaf

350 ml/12 fl oz tomato juice, plus extra if needed

2–3 tbsp chopped fresh dill, plus extra sprigs to garnish

fresh lemon juice (optional)

salt and pepper

soured cream or yogurt, to garnish

Oriental Duck Broth

Put the duck in a large saucepan with the water. Bring just to the boil and skim off the scum that rises to the surface. Add the stock, ginger, carrot, onion, leek, garlic, peppercorns and soy sauce. Reduce the heat and simmer, partially covered, for 1½ hours.

Remove the duck from the stock and set aside. When the duck is cool enough to handle, remove the meat from the bones and slice thinly or shred into bite-sized pieces, discarding any fat.

Strain the stock and press with the back of a spoon to extract all the liquid. Remove as much fat as possible. Discard the vegetables and herbs.

Bring the stock just to the boil in a clean saucepan and add the strips of carrot and leek, the mushrooms and duck meat. Reduce the heat and cook gently for 5 minutes, or until the carrot is just tender.

Stir in the watercress and continue simmering for 1–2 minutes until it is wilted. Taste the soup and adjust the seasoning if needed, adding a little more soy sauce if wished. Ladle the soup into warmed bowls and serve immediately.

SERVES 4–6

2 duck leg quarters, skinned

1 litre/1³/₄ pints water

600 ml/1 pint chicken stock

2.5-cm/1-inch piece fresh root ginger, sliced

1 large carrot, sliced

1 onion, sliced

1 leek, sliced

3 garlic cloves, crushed

l tsp black peppercorns

2 tbsp soy sauce, or to taste

l small carrot, cut into thin strips or slivers

l small leek, cut into thin strips or slivers

100 g/3¹/₂ oz shiitake mushrooms, thinly sliced

25 g/1 oz watercress leaves

salt and pepper

Beef Broth with Herbs & Vegetables

Preheat the oven to 190°C/375°F/Gas Mark 5. To make the stock, trim as much fat as possible from the beef and put in a large roasting tin with the bones and onions. Roast in a preheated oven for 30–40 minutes until browned, turning once or twice. Transfer the ingredients to a large flameproof casserole and discard the fat.

Add the water (it should cover by at least 5 cm/2 inches) and bring to the boil. Skim off any scum that rises to the surface. Reduce the heat and add the garlic, carrots, leek, celery, bay leaf, thyme and a pinch of salt. Simmer very gently, uncovered, for 4 hours, skimming occasionally. Do not stir. If the ingredients emerge from the liquid, top up with water.

Gently ladle the stock through a muslin-lined sieve into a large container and remove as much fat as possible. Save the meat for another purpose, if wished, and discard the bones and vegetables. (There should be about 2 litres/3½ pints of stock.)

Boil the stock very gently until it is reduced to 1.5 litres/2¾ pints, or if the stock already has concentrated flavour, measure out that amount and save the rest for another purpose. Taste the stock and adjust the seasoning if necessary.

Bring a saucepan of salted water to the boil and drop in the celeriac and carrots. Reduce the heat, cover and boil gently for about 15 minutes until tender. Drain.

Add the marjoram and parsley to the boiling beef stock. Divide the cooked vegetables and diced tomatoes among warmed bowls, ladle over the boiling stock and serve.

SERVES 4–6

200 g/7 oz celeriac, peeled and finely diced

2 large carrots, finely diced

2 tsp chopped fresh marjoram leaves

2 tsp chopped fresh parsley

2 plum tomatoes, skinned, deseeded and diced

salt and pepper

beef stock

550 g/1 lb 4 oz boneless beef shin or stewing steak, cut into large cubes

750 g/1 lb 10 oz veal, beef or pork bones

2 onions, quartered

2.5 litres/4¹/₃ pints water

4 garlic cloves, sliced

2 carrots, sliced

1 large leek, sliced

1 celery stick, cut into 5-cm/ 2.5-inch pieces

1 bay leaf

4–5 sprigs of fresh thyme, or ¹/₄ tsp dried thyme

salt

Fennel & Tomato Soup with Prawns

Heat the olive oil in a large saucepan over a medium heat. Add the onion and fennel and cook for 3–4 minutes, stirring occasionally, until the onion is just softened.

Add the potato, water, tomato juice and bay leaf with a large pinch of salt. Reduce the heat, cover and simmer for about 25 minutes, stirring once or twice, until the vegetables are soft.

Allow the soup to cool slightly, then transfer to a food processor or blender and process until smooth, working in batches if necessary. (If using a food processor, strain off the cooking liquid and reserve. Purée the soup solids with enough cooking liquid to moisten them, then combine with the remaining liquid.)

Return the soup to the saucepan and add the prawns. Simmer gently for about 10 minutes, to reheat the soup and allow it to absorb the prawn flavour.

Stir in the tomatoes and dill. Taste and adjust the seasoning, adding salt, if needed, and pepper. Thin the soup with a little more tomato juice, if wished. Ladle into warmed bowls, garnish with dill or fennel fronds and serve.

SERVES 4

2 tsp olive oil

1 large onion, halved and sliced

2 large fennel bulbs, halved and sliced

1 small potato, diced

850 ml/1^1/$_2$ pints water

400 ml/14 fl oz tomato juice, plus extra if needed

1 bay leaf

125 g/4^1/$_2$ oz cooked peeled small prawns

2 tomatoes, skinned, deseeded and chopped

^{1}/$_2$ tsp snipped fresh dill

salt and pepper

dill sprigs or fennel fronds, to garnish

Salmon & Leek Soup

Heat the oil in a heavy-based saucepan over a medium heat. Add the onion and leeks and cook for about 3 minutes until they begin to soften.

Add the potato, stock, water and bay leaf with a large pinch of salt. Bring to the boil, reduce the heat, cover and cook gently for about 25 minutes until the vegetables are tender. Remove the bay leaf.

Allow the soup to cool slightly, then transfer about half of it to a food processor or blender and process until smooth. (If using a food processor, strain off the cooking liquid and reserve. Purée half the soup solids with enough cooking liquid to moisten them, then combine with the remaining liquid.)

Return the puréed soup to the saucepan and stir to blend. Reheat gently over a medium-low heat.

Season the salmon with salt and pepper and add to the soup. Continue cooking for about 5 minutes, stirring occasionally, until the fish is tender and starts to break up. Stir in the cream, taste and adjust the seasoning, adding a little lemon juice if wished. Ladle into warmed bowls, garnish with chervil or parsley and serve.

SERVES 4

1 tbsp olive oil

1 large onion, finely chopped

3 large leeks, including green parts, thinly sliced

1 potato, finely diced

450 ml/16 fl oz fish stock

700 ml/$1^1/_4$ pints water

1 bay leaf

300 g/$10^1/_2$ oz skinless salmon fillet, cut into 1-cm/$^1/_2$-inch cubes

80 ml/3 fl oz double cream

fresh lemon juice (optional)

salt and pepper

sprigs of fresh chervil or parsley, to garnish

Genoese Fish Soup

Melt the butter in a large, heavy-based saucepan. Add the onion and garlic and cook over a low heat, stirring occasionally, for 5 minutes, or until softened.

Add the streaky bacon and celery and cook, stirring frequently, for a further 2 minutes.

Add the tomatoes, wine, stock, basil and 1 tablespoon of the parsley. Season to taste with salt and pepper. Bring to the boil, then reduce the heat and simmer for 10 minutes.

Add the fish and cook for 5 minutes, or until it is opaque. Add the prawns and heat through gently for 3 minutes. Ladle into warmed serving bowls, garnish with the remaining chopped parsley and serve immediately.

SERVES 4

25 g/1 oz butter

1 onion, chopped

1 garlic clove, finely chopped

55 g/2 oz rindless streaky bacon, diced

2 celery sticks, chopped

400 g/14 oz canned chopped tomatoes

150 ml/5 fl oz dry white wine

300 ml/10 fl oz fish stock

4 fresh basil leaves, torn

2 tbsp chopped fresh flat-leaf parsley

450 g/1 lb white fish fillets, such as cod or monkfish, skinned and chopped

115 g/4 oz cooked peeled prawns

salt and pepper

5

Luxury Soups

This section contains a range of decadent dishes for those times when you want to impress your friends or just to indulge yourself. Mushroom & Sherry Soup and Lobster Bisque are sure to hit the spot and you should not miss Cold Cucumber & Smoked Salmon Soup or Creamy Oyster Soup. These are truly 'super soups' and are well worth experimenting with to the delight of your family and friends.

Mushroom & Sherry Soup

Melt the butter in a large saucepan over a low heat. Add the garlic and onions and cook, stirring, for 3 minutes, until slightly softened. Add the mushrooms and cook for a further 5 minutes, stirring. Add the chopped parsley, pour in the stock and season with salt and pepper. Bring to the boil, then reduce the heat, cover the pan and simmer for 20 minutes.

Put the flour into a bowl, mix in enough milk to make a smooth paste, then stir it into the soup. Cook, stirring, for 5 minutes. Stir in the remaining milk and the sherry and cook for a further 5 minutes. Remove from the heat and stir in the soured cream. Return the pan to the heat and warm gently.

Remove from the heat and ladle into serving bowls. Garnish with chopped fresh parsley and serve immediately.

SERVES 4

4 tbsp butter

2 garlic cloves, chopped

3 onions, sliced

450 g/1 lb mixed white and chestnut mushrooms, sliced

100 g/3^1/$_2$ oz fresh ceps or porcini mushrooms, sliced

3 tbsp chopped fresh parsley, plus extra to garnish

500 ml/18 fl oz vegetable stock

3 tbsp plain flour

125 ml/4 fl oz milk

2 tbsp sherry

125 ml/4 fl oz soured cream

salt and pepper

Celery & Stilton Soup

Melt the butter in a large saucepan over a medium-low heat. Add the onion and cook for 3–4 minutes, stirring frequently, until just softened. Add the celery and carrot and continue cooking for 3 minutes. Season lightly with salt and pepper.

Add the stock, thyme and bay leaf and bring to the boil. Reduce the heat, cover and simmer gently for about 25 minutes, stirring occasionally, until the vegetables are very tender.

Allow the soup to cool slightly and remove the thyme and bay leaf. Transfer the soup to a food processor or blender and process until smooth, working in batches, if necessary. (If using a food processor, strain off the cooking liquid and reserve. Purée the soup solids with enough cooking liquid to moisten them, then combine with the remaining liquid.)

Return the puréed soup to the rinsed-out saucepan and stir in the cream. Simmer over a low heat for 5 minutes.

Add the Stilton slowly, stirring constantly, until smooth. (Do not allow the soup to boil.) Taste and adjust the seasoning, adding salt, if needed, plenty of pepper and nutmeg to taste.

Ladle into warmed bowls, garnish with celery leaves and serve.

SERVES 4

2 tbsp butter

1 onion, finely chopped

4 large celery sticks, finely chopped

1 large carrot, finely chopped

1 litre/$1^3/4$ pints chicken or
   vegetable stock

3–4 thyme sprigs

1 bay leaf

125 ml/4 fl oz double cream

150 g/$5^1/2$ oz Stilton cheese,
   crumbled

freshly grated nutmeg

salt and pepper

celery leaves, to garnish

White Bean Soup with Olive Tapenade

Pick over the beans, cover generously with cold water and leave to soak for 6 hours or overnight. Drain the beans, put in a saucepan and add cold water to cover by 5 cm/2 inches. Bring to the boil and boil for 10 minutes. Drain and rinse well.

Heat the oil in a large heavy-based saucepan over a medium heat. Add the onion and leek, cover and cook for 3–4 minutes, stirring occasionally, until just softened. Add the garlic, celery, carrots and fennel, and continue cooking for 2 minutes.

Add the water, drained beans and the herbs. When the mixture begins to bubble, reduce the heat to low. Cover and simmer gently, stirring occasionally, for about 1½ hours, until the beans are very tender.

Meanwhile make the tapenade. Put the garlic, parsley and drained olives in a food processor or blender with the olive oil. Blend to a purée and scrape into a small serving bowl.

Allow the soup to cool slightly, then transfer to a food procesor or blender and process until smooth, working in batches if necessary. (If using a food processor, strain off the cooking liquid and reserve. Purée the soup solids with enough cooking liquid to moisten them, then combine with the remaining liquid.)

Return the puréed soup to the rinsed-out saucepan and thin with a little water, if necessary. Season with salt and pepper to taste, and simmer until heated through. Ladle into warmed bowls and serve, stirring a generous teaspoon of the tapenade into each serving.

SERVES 8

350 g/12 oz dried haricot beans

1 tbsp olive oil

1 large onion, finely chopped

1 large leek (white part only), thinly sliced

3 garlic cloves, finely chopped

2 celery sticks, finely chopped

2 small carrots, finely chopped

1 small fennel bulb, finely chopped

2 litres/3^1/$_2$ pints water

^{1}/$_4$ tsp dried thyme

^{1}/$_4$ tsp dried marjoram

salt and pepper

tapenade

1 garlic clove

1 small bunch fresh flat-leaf parsley, stems removed

240 g/8^1/$_2$ oz almond-stuffed green olives, drained

5 tbsp olive oil

Chestnut Soup

Melt the butter in a large saucepan over a medium heat. Add the onion and celery and cook for 4–5 minutes, until softened.

Add the chestnuts and sauté for a further 5 minutes.

Pour in the stock and mix well. Bring to the boil and simmer for 20–25 minutes, until the chestnuts are tender.

Transfer to a food processor or blender and process until smooth. Return to the rinsed-out saucepan.

Add the cream to the soup, reheat and season to taste with salt and pepper.

Add the sherry, if using, and serve in warmed bowls garnished with the parsley.

SERVES 6

25 g/1 oz butter or 1 tbsp olive oil

1 onion, finely chopped

1 celery stick, chopped

200 g/7 oz vacuum-packed whole chestnuts

1 litre/$1^3/_4$ pints chicken or vegetable stock

125 ml/4 fl oz single cream

2 tbsp sherry (optional)

salt and pepper

chopped fresh parsley, to garnish

Vichyssoise

Trim the leeks and remove most of the green part. Slice the white part of the leeks very finely.

Melt the butter in a saucepan. Add the leeks and onion and fry, stirring occasionally, for about 5 minutes without browning.

Add the potatoes, stock, lemon juice, nutmeg, coriander and bay leaf to the pan, season to taste with salt and pepper and bring to the boil. Cover and simmer for about 30 minutes, until all the vegetables are very soft.

Cool the soup a little, remove and discard the bay leaf and then press through a strainer or process in a food processor or blender until smooth. Pour into a clean pan.

Blend the egg yolk into the cream, add a little of the soup to the mixture and then whisk it all back into the soup and reheat gently, without boiling. Adjust the seasoning to taste. Cool and then chill thoroughly in the refrigerator.

Serve the soup sprinkled with freshly snipped chives.

SERVES 6

3 large leeks

40 g/1^1/$_2$ oz butter or margarine

1 onion, thinly sliced

500 g/1 lb 2 oz potatoes, chopped

850 ml/1^1/$_2$ pints vegetable stock

2 tsp lemon juice

pinch of ground nutmeg

^{1}/$_4$ tsp ground coriander

1 bay leaf

1 egg yolk

150 ml/5 fl oz single cream

salt and white pepper

freshly snipped chives, to garnish

Bloody Mary Soup

Pour the tomatoes and stock into a saucepan and cook with the garlic and basil for 3–4 minutes.

Transfer to a food processor or blender and process until smooth. Return to the rinsed-out saucepan.

Season to taste with salt and pepper, Worcestershire sauce and Tabasco.

Stir in the vodka and serve in small bowls garnished with the parsley. This soup can also be served cold.

SERVES 4

400 g/14 oz canned chopped
    tomatoes
350 ml/12 fl oz chicken stock
2 garlic cloves, crushed
small handful of basil leaves
Worcestershire sauce
Tabasco sauce
4 tbsp vodka
salt and pepper
sprigs of fresh flat-leaf parsley,
    to garnish

Chicken Ravioli in Tarragon Broth

To make the pasta, combine the flour, tarragon and a pinch of salt in a food processor. Beat together the egg, egg yolk, oil and 2 tablespoons of the water. With the machine running, pour in the egg mixture and process until it forms a ball, leaving the sides of the bowl virtually clean. If the dough is crumbly, add the remaining water; if the dough is sticky, add 1–2 tablespoons flour and continue kneading in the food processor until a ball forms. Wrap and chill for at least 30 minutes. Reserve the egg white.

To make the filling, put the chicken, lemon rind and mixed herbs in a food processor and season with salt and pepper. Chop finely, by pulsing; do not overprocess. Scrape into a bowl and stir in the cream. Taste and adjust the seasoning, if necessary.

Divide the pasta dough in half. Cover one half and roll the other half on a floured surface as thinly as possible, less than 1.5 mm/$\frac{1}{16}$ inch. Cut out rectangles measuring about 10 x 5 cm/4 x 2 inches.

Place rounded teaspoons of filling on one half of the dough pieces. Brush around the edges with egg white and fold in half. Press the edges gently but firmly to seal. Arrange the ravioli in one layer on a baking sheet, dusted generously with flour. Repeat with the remaining dough. Allow the ravioli to dry in a cool place for about 15 minutes or chill for 1–2 hours.

Bring a large quantity of water to the boil. Drop in half the ravioli and cook for 12–15 minutes, until just tender. Drain on a clean tea towel while cooking the remainder.

Meanwhile, put the stock and tarragon in a large saucepan. Bring to the boil and reduce the heat to bubble very gently. Cover and simmer for about 15 minutes, to infuse. Add the cooked ravioli and simmer for a further 5 minutes. Ladle into warmed soup bowls to serve with the Parmesan cheese.

SERVES 6

2 litres/3$\frac{1}{2}$ pints chicken stock

2 tbsp finely chopped fresh tarragon leaves

freshly grated Parmesan cheese, to serve

pasta dough

125 g/4$\frac{1}{2}$ oz flour, plus extra if needed

2 tbsp fresh tarragon leaves, stems removed

1 egg

1 egg, separated

1 tsp extra virgin olive oil

2–3 tbsp water

salt

filling

200 g/7 oz cooked chicken, coarsely chopped

$\frac{1}{2}$ tsp grated lemon rind

2 tbsp chopped mixed fresh tarragon, chives and parsley

4 tbsp whipping cream

salt and pepper

Turkey Soup with Rice, Mushrooms & Sage

Melt half the butter in a large saucepan over a medium-low heat. Add the onion, celery and sage and cook for 3–4 minutes, until the onion is softened, stirring frequently. Stir in the flour and continue cooking for 2 minutes.

Slowly add about one quarter of the stock and stir well, scraping the bottom of the pan to mix in the flour. Pour in the remaining stock, stirring to combine completely, and bring just to the boil.

Stir in the rice and season with salt and pepper. Reduce the heat and simmer gently, partially covered, for about 30 minutes until the rice is just tender, stirring occasionally.

Meanwhile, melt the remaining butter in a large frying pan over a medium heat. Add the mushrooms and season with salt and pepper. Cook for about 8 minutes, until they are golden brown, stirring occasionally at first, then more often after they start to colour. Add the mushrooms to the soup.

Add the turkey to the soup and stir in the cream. Continue simmering for about 10 minutes, until heated through. Taste and adjust the seasoning, if necessary. Ladle into warmed bowls, garnish with sage and serve with Parmesan cheese.

SERVES 4–5

3 tbsp butter

1 onion, finely chopped

1 celery stick, finely chopped

25 large fresh sage leaves, finely chopped

4 tbsp plain flour

1.2 litres/2 pints turkey or chicken stock

100 g/3^1/$_2$ oz brown rice

250 g/9 oz mushrooms, sliced

200 g/7 oz cooked turkey

200 ml/7 fl oz double cream

salt and pepper

sprigs of fresh sage, to garnish

freshly grated Parmesan cheese, to serve

Oriental Pork Balls & Greens in Broth

To make the pork balls, put the pork, spinach, spring onions and garlic in a bowl. Add the 5-spice powder and soy sauce and mix until combined.

Shape the pork mixture into 24 balls. Place them in one layer in a steamer that will fit over the top of a saucepan.

Bring the stock just to the boil in a saucepan that will accommodate the steamer. Regulate the heat so that the liquid bubbles gently. Add the mushrooms to the stock and place the steamer, covered, on top of the pan. Steam for 10 minutes. Remove the steamer and set aside on a plate.

Add the pak choy and spring onions to the pan and cook gently in the stock for 3–4 minutes, or until the leaves are wilted. Taste the soup and adjust the seasoning, if necessary.

Divide the pork balls evenly among 6 warmed bowls and ladle the soup over them. Serve immediately.

SERVES 6

2 litres/$3^1/_2$ pints chicken stock

85 g/3 oz shiitake mushrooms, thinly sliced

175 g/6 oz pak choy or other Oriental greens, sliced into thin ribbons

6 spring onions, finely sliced

salt and pepper

pork balls

225 g/8 oz fresh lean pork mince

25 g/1 oz fresh spinach leaves, finely chopped

2 spring onions, finely chopped

1 garlic clove, very finely chopped

pinch of Oriental 5-spice powder

1 tsp soy sauce

Consommé

Put the stock and minced beef in a saucepan and leave for 1 hour. Add the tomatoes, carrots, onion, celery, turnip (if using), bouquet garni, 2 of the egg whites, the crushed shells of 2 of the eggs and plenty of seasoning. Bring almost to boiling point, whisking hard all the time with a flat whisk.

Cover and simmer for 1 hour, taking care not to allow the layer of froth on top of the soup to break.

Pour the soup through a jelly bag or scalded fine cloth, keeping the froth back until the last, then pour the ingredients through the cloth again into a clean pan. The resulting liquid should be clear.

If the soup is not quite clear, return it to the pan with another egg white and the crushed shells of 2 more eggs. Repeat the whisking process as before and then boil for 10 minutes; strain again.

Add the sherry, if using, to the soup and reheat gently. Place the garnish in the warmed soup bowls and carefully pour in the soup. Serve immediately.

SERVES 4–6

1.25 litres/2$\frac{1}{4}$ pints strong beef stock

225 g/8 oz fresh extra lean beef mince

2 tomatoes, skinned, seeded and chopped

2 large carrots, chopped

1 large onion, chopped

2 celery sticks, chopped

1 turnip, chopped (optional)

1 bouquet garni

2–3 egg whites

shells of 2–4 eggs, crushed

1–2 tbsp sherry (optional)

salt and pepper

julienne strips of raw carrot, turnip, celery or celeriac, to garnish

Lemon Veal Soup with Mushrooms

Put the veal in a large saucepan and add the stock. Bring just to the boil and skim off any scum that rises to the surface.

Add the onion, carrots, garlic, lemon rind and bay leaf. Season with salt and pepper. Reduce the heat and simmer, partially covered, for about 45 minutes, stirring occasionally, until the veal is very tender.

Remove the veal and carrots with a slotted spoon and reserve, covered. Strain the stock into a clean saucepan. Discard the onion and garlic, lemon rind and bay leaf.

Melt the butter in a frying pan over a medium-high heat. Add the mushrooms, season, and fry gently until lightly golden. Reserve with the veal and carrots.

Mix together the cornflour and cream. Bring the cooking liquid just to the boil and whisk in the cream mixture. Boil very gently for 2–3 minutes until it thickens, whisking almost constantly.

Add the reserved meat and vegetables to the soup and simmer over a low heat for about 5 minutes until heated through. Taste and adjust the seasoning, adding nutmeg and a squeeze of lemon juice, if using. Stir in the parsley, then ladle into warmed bowls and serve.

SERVES 4

350 g/12 oz boneless veal, cut into 1-cm/^{1}/$_2$-inch pieces

1 litre/1^3/$_4$ pints chicken stock

l onion, quartered

2 carrots, thinly sliced

2 garlic cloves, halved

1 pared strip lemon rind

1 bay leaf

1 tbsp butter

350 g/12 oz small button mushrooms, quartered

4 tbsp cornflour

125 ml/4 fl oz double cream

freshly grated nutmeg

fresh lemon juice, to taste (optional)

1–2 tbsp chopped fresh parsley

salt and pepper

Cold Cucumber & Smoked Salmon Soup

Heat the oil in a large saucepan over a medium heat. Add the onion and cook for about 3 minutes, until it begins to soften.

Add the cucumber, potato, celery and stock, along with a large pinch of salt, if using unsalted stock. Bring to the boil, reduce the heat, cover and cook gently for about 20 minutes until the vegetables are tender.

Allow the soup to cool slightly, then transfer to a food processor or blender, working in batches if necessary. Purée the soup until smooth. (If using a food processor, strain off the cooking liquid and reserve it. Purée the soup solids with enough cooking liquid to moisten them, then combine with the remaining liquid.)

Transfer the puréed soup into a large container. Cover and refrigerate until cold.

Stir the cream, salmon and chives into the soup. If time permits, chill for at least 1 hour to allow the flavours to blend. Taste and adjust the seasoning, adding salt, if needed, and pepper. Ladle into chilled bowls and serve.

SERVES 4

2 tsp oil

1 large onion, finely chopped

1 large cucumber, peeled, deseeded and sliced

1 small potato, diced

1 celery stick, finely chopped

1 litre/$1^3/_4$ pints chicken or vegetable stock

150 ml/5 fl oz double cream

150 g/$5^1/_2$ oz smoked salmon, finely diced

2 tbsp snipped fresh chives

salt and pepper

Bouillabaisse

Heat the oil in a large pan over a medium heat. Add the garlic and onions and cook, stirring, for 3 minutes. Stir in the tomatoes, stock, wine, bay leaf, saffron and herbs. Bring to the boil, reduce the heat, cover and simmer for 30 minutes.

Meanwhile, soak the mussels in lightly salted water for 10 minutes. Scrub the shells under cold running water and pull off any beards. Discard any mussels with broken shells or any that refuse to close when tapped. Put the rest into a large pan with a little water, bring to the boil and cook over a high heat for 4 minutes. Remove from the heat and discard any that remain closed.

When the tomato mixture is cooked, rinse the fish fillets, pat dry and cut into chunks. Add to the pan and simmer for 5 minutes. Add the mussels, prawns and scallops and season with salt and pepper. Cook for 3 minutes, until the fish is cooked through. Remove from the heat, discard the bay leaf and ladle into serving bowls.

SERVES 4

100 ml/$3^1/2$ fl oz olive oil

3 garlic cloves, chopped

2 onions, chopped

2 tomatoes, deseeded and chopped

700 ml/$1^1/4$ pints fish stock

400 ml/14 fl oz white wine

1 bay leaf

pinch of saffron threads

2 tbsp chopped fresh basil

2 tbsp chopped fresh parsley

200 g/7 oz live mussels

250 g/9 oz snapper or monkfish fillets

250 g/9 oz haddock fillets, skinned

200 g/7 oz prawns, peeled and deveined

100 g/$3^1/2$ oz scallops

salt and pepper

Seared Scallops in Garlic Broth

Combine the garlic cloves, celery, carrot, onion, peppercorns, parsley stems and water in a saucepan with a good pinch of salt. Bring to the boil, reduce the heat and simmer, partially covered, for 30–45 minutes.

Strain the stock into a clean saucepan. Taste and adjust the seasoning, and keep hot.

If using sea scallops, slice in half horizontally to form 2 thinner rounds from each. (If the scallops are very large, slice them into 3 rounds.) Sprinkle with salt and pepper.

Heat the oil in a frying pan over a medium-high heat and cook the scallops on one side for 1–2 minutes, until lightly browned and the flesh becomes opaque.

Divide the scallops between 4 warmed shallow bowls, arranging them browned-side up. Ladle the soup over the scallops, then float a few coriander leaves on top. Serve immediately.

SERVES 4

1 large garlic bulb (about 100 g/ 3^1/$_2$ oz), separated into unpeeled cloves

1 celery stick, chopped

1 carrot, chopped

1 onion, chopped

10 peppercorns

5–6 parsley stems

1.2 litres/2 pints water

225 g/8 oz large sea scallops or queen scallops

1 tbsp oil

salt and pepper

fresh coriander leaves, to garnish

Saffron Mussel Soup

Discard any mussels with broken shells or any that refuse to close when tapped. Rinse, pull off any beards, and if there are barnacles, scrape them off with a knife under cold running water.

Put the mussels in a large heavy-based saucepan over a high heat with the wine and a little pepper. Cover tightly and cook for 4–5 minutes, or until the mussels open, shaking the pan occasionally. Discard any that remain closed.

When they are cool enough to handle, remove the mussels from the shells, adding any additional juices to the cooking liquid. Strain the cooking liquid through a muslin-lined sieve. Top up the cooking liquid with water to make 1 litre/1¾ pints.

Melt the butter in heavy-based saucepan. Add the shallots and leek, cover and cook until they begin to soften, stirring occasionally.

Stir in the mussel cooking liquid and the saffron. Bring to the boil, reduce the heat and simmer for 15–20 minutes, until the vegetables are very tender.

Add the cream, stir and bring just to the boil. Stir the dissolved cornflour into the soup and boil gently for 2–3 minutes, until slightly thickened, stirring frequently. Add the mussels and cook for 1–2 minutes to reheat them. Taste and adjust the seasoning, if necessary. Stir in the parsley, ladle into warmed bowls and serve.

SERVES 4–6

2 kg/4 lb 8 oz live mussels

150 ml/5 fl oz dry white wine

1 tbsp butter

2 large shallots, finely chopped

1 leek, halved lengthways and thinly sliced

pinch of saffron threads

300 ml/10 fl oz double cream

1 tbsp cornflour, dissolved in 2 tbsp water

2 tbsp chopped fresh parsley

salt and pepper

Squid, Chorizo & Tomato Soup

Cut off the squid tentacles and cut into bite-sized pieces. Slice the bodies into rings.

Place a large saucepan over a medium-low heat and add the chorizo. Cook for 5–10 minutes, stirring frequently, until it renders most of its fat. Remove with a slotted spoon and drain on paper towels.

Pour off all the fat from the pan and add the onion, celery, carrot and garlic. Cover and cook for 3–4 minutes, until the onion is slightly softened.

Stir in the tomatoes, fish stock, cumin, saffron, bay leaf and chorizo.

Add the squid to the soup. Bring almost to the boil, reduce the heat, cover and cook gently for 40–45 minutes, or until the squid and carrot are tender, stirring occasionally.

Taste the soup and stir in a little chilli purée for a spicier flavour, if using. Season with salt and pepper. Ladle into warmed bowls, sprinkle with parsley and serve.

SERVES 6

450 g/1 lb cleaned squid

150 g/5^1/$_2$ oz lean chorizo, peeled and very finely diced

1 onion, finely chopped

1 celery stick, thinly sliced

1 carrot, thinly sliced

2 garlic cloves, finely chopped or crushed

400 g/14 oz canned chopped tomatoes

1.2 litres/2 pints fish stock

^{1}/$_2$ tsp ground cumin

pinch of saffron

1 bay leaf

chilli purée (optional)

salt and pepper

fresh chopped parsley, to garnish

Lobster Bisque

Pull off the lobster tail. With the legs up, cut the body in half lengthways. Scoop out the tomalley (the soft pale greenish-grey part) and, if it is a female, the roe (the solid red-orange part). Reserve these together, covered and refrigerated. Remove the meat and cut into bite-sized pieces; cover and refrigerate. Chop the shell into large pieces.

Melt half the butter in a large saucepan over a medium heat and add the lobster shell pieces. Fry until brown bits begin to stick on the bottom of the pan. Add the carrot, celery, leek, onion and shallots. Cook, stirring, for 1½–2 minutes (do not allow to burn). Add the brandy and wine and bubble for 1 minute. Pour over the water, add the tomato purée, a large pinch of salt and bring to the boil. Reduce the heat, simmer for 30 minutes and strain the stock, discarding the solids.

Melt the remaining butter in a small saucepan and add the tomalley and roe, if any. Add the cream, whisk to mix well, remove from the heat and set aside.

Put the flour in a small mixing bowl and very slowly whisk in the cold water. Stir in a little of the hot stock mixture to make a smooth liquid.

Bring the remaining lobster stock to the boil and whisk in the flour mixture. Boil gently for 4–5 minutes until the soup thickens, stirring frequently. Press the tomalley, roe and cream mixture through a sieve into the soup. Reduce the heat and add the reserved lobster meat. Simmer gently until heated through.

Taste the soup and adjust the seasoning, adding more cream if wished. Ladle into warmed bowls, sprinkle with chives and serve.

SERVES 4

450 g/1 lb cooked lobster
45 g/1½ oz butter
1 small carrot, grated
1 celery stick, finely chopped
1 leek, finely chopped
1 small onion, finely chopped
2 shallots, finely chopped
3 tbsp brandy or Cognac
55 ml/2 fl oz dry white wine
1.2 litres/2 pints water
1 tbsp tomato purée
125 ml/4 fl oz whipping cream, or to taste
6 tbsp plain flour
2–3 tbsp water
salt and pepper
snipped fresh chives, to garnish

Creamy Oyster Soup

To open the oysters, hold flat-side up, over a sieve set over a bowl to catch the juices, and push an oyster knife into the hinge. Work it around until you can prise off the top shell. When all the oysters have been opened, strain the liquid through a sieve lined with damp muslin. Remove any bits of shell stuck to the oysters and reserve them in their liquid.

Melt half the butter in a saucepan over a low heat. Add the shallots and cook gently for about 5 minutes, until just softened, stirring frequently; do not allow them to brown.

Add the wine, bring to the boil and boil for 1 minute. Stir in the fish stock, bring back to the boil and boil for 3–4 minutes. Reduce the heat to a gentle simmer.

Add the oysters and their liquid and poach for about 1 minute, until they become more firm but are still tender. Remove the oysters with a slotted spoon and reserve, covered. Strain the stock.

Bring the strained stock to the boil in a clean saucepan. Add the cream and bring back to the boil.

Stir the dissolved cornflour into the soup and boil gently for 2–3 minutes, stirring frequently, until slightly thickened. Add the oysters and cook for 1–2 minutes to reheat them. Taste and adjust the seasoning, if necessary, and ladle the soup into warmed bowls. Top each serving with a teaspoon of caviar or roe, if using.

SERVES 4

12 oysters
2 tbsp butter
2 shallots, finely chopped
5 tbsp white wine
300 ml/10 fl oz fish stock
175 ml/6 fl oz whipping or double cream
2 tbsp cornflour, dissolved in 2 tbsp cold water
salt and pepper
caviar or lumpfish roe, to garnish (optional)

6

Accompaniments

Freshly-baked bread is the perfect partner for home-made soup – it is ideal for dunking and for mopping up the last delicious drops. Any leftover bread can be used to make croûtons – fried cubes of bread – adding taste and crunch. Croûtons can even be made in a variety of flavours, such as garlic, chilli or herb, to perfectly complement the soup they are accompanying.

Croûtons

Cut the bread into 1-cm/^{1}/$_2$-inch cubes.

Heat the oil in a frying pan and add the garlic, if using, and bread cubes in a single layer, tossing occasionally, until the bread is golden brown and crisp.

Remove the pan from the heat and spoon out the croûtons onto kitchen paper to drain.

Whilst the croûtons are still hot, toss them in the fresh herbs, paprika or Parmesan, if using. Season to taste with salt and pepper.

The croûtons are best used on the day of making.

SERVES 4–6

2 slices day-old white, wholemeal or granary bread, crusts removed

4 tbsp vegetable or olive oil

1 garlic clove, finely chopped (optional)

finely chopped fresh herbs, such as parsley and thyme (optional)

^{1}/$_2$ teaspoon paprika or chilli powder (optional)

1 tbsp freshly grated Parmesan cheese (optional)

salt and pepper

White Bread

Mix the flour, salt and yeast together in a mixing bowl. Add the oil and water and stir well to form a soft dough.

Turn the dough out onto a lightly floured board and knead well by hand for 5–7 minutes. Alternatively, use a free-standing electric mixer for this and knead the dough with the dough hook for 4–5 minutes. The dough should have a smooth appearance and feel elastic.

Return the dough to the bowl, cover with clingfilm and leave to rise in a warm place for 1 hour. When it has doubled in size, turn it out onto a floured board and knead again for 30 seconds; this is known as 'knocking back'. Knead it until smooth.

Shape the dough into a rectangle the length of a 900-g/2-lb loaf tin and three times the width. Grease the tin well, fold the dough into three lengthways and put it in the tin with the join underneath for a well-shaped loaf. Cover and leave to rise in a warm place for 30 minutes, until it has risen well above the tin. Meanwhile, preheat the oven to 220°C/425°F/Gas Mark 7.

Bake in the centre of the preheated oven for 25–30 minutes, until firm and golden brown. Test that the loaf is cooked by tapping it on the bottom – it should sound hollow. Cool on a cooling rack for 30 minutes. Store in an airtight container in a cool place for 3–4 days.

MAKES 1 LARGE LOAF

450 g/1 lb strong white flour, plus extra for dusting

1 tsp salt

7 g/¼ oz easy-blend dried yeast

1 tbsp vegetable oil or melted butter, plus extra for greasing

300 ml/10 fl oz warm water

Walnut & Seed Bread

In a mixing bowl, mix together the flours, seeds, walnuts, salt and yeast. Add the oil and warm water and stir well to form a soft dough.

Turn the dough out onto a lightly floured board and knead well for 5–7 minutes. The dough should have a smooth appearance and feel elastic.

Return the dough to the bowl, cover with a clean cloth or clingfilm and leave in a warm place for 1–1½ hours to rise. On top of the boiler, on an Aga or in an airing cupboard works well.

When the dough has doubled in size, turn it out onto a lightly floured board and knead again for 1 minute.

Grease two 900-g/2-lb loaf tins well with melted butter or oil. Divide the dough into two. Shape one piece into a rectangle the length of the tin and three times the width. Fold the dough into three lengthways. Place in one of the tins with the join underneath for a well-shaped loaf. Repeat with the other piece of dough.

Cover and leave to rise again in a warm place for about 30 minutes, until the bread is well risen above the tins. Meanwhile, preheat the oven to 230°C/450°F/Gas Mark 8.

Bake in the centre of the preheated oven, for 25–30 minutes. If the loaves are getting too brown, reduce the temperature to 220°C/425°F/Gas Mark 7. To test that the bread is cooked, tap the loaf on the bottom – it should sound hollow.

Cool on a cooling rack for 30 minutes to 1 hour; this enables the steam to escape and prevents a soggy loaf. When cool, seal in a plastic bag and keep in the refrigerator for up to 1 week.

MAKES 2 LARGE LOAVES

450 g/1 lb wholemeal flour

450 g/1 lb granary flour

115 g/4 oz strong white flour, plus extra for dusting

2 tbsp sesame seeds

2 tbsp sunflower seeds

2 tbsp poppy seeds

115 g/4 oz walnuts, chopped

2 tsp salt

15 g/½ oz easy-blend dried yeast

2 tbsp olive oil or walnut oil

700 ml/1¼ pints warm water

1 tbsp melted butter or oil, for greasing

Irish Soda Bread

Preheat the oven to 230°C/450°F/Gas Mark 8, then dust a baking sheet with flour. Sift the white flour, wholemeal flour, bicarbonate of soda and salt into a bowl and stir in the sugar. Make a well in the centre and pour in enough of the buttermilk to make a dough that is soft but not too wet and sticky. Add a little more buttermilk, if necessary.

Turn the dough out onto a floured work surface and knead very briefly into a large round 5 cm/2 inches thick. Dust lightly with flour and, using a sharp knife, mark the top of the loaf with a deep cross.

Place the loaf on the baking sheet and bake in the preheated oven for 15 minutes. Reduce the oven temperature to 200°C/400°F/Gas Mark 6 and bake for a further 20–25 minutes, or until the loaf sounds hollow when tapped on the bottom. Transfer to a wire rack to cool, and eat while still warm.

MAKES 1 LOAF

280 g/10 oz plain white flour,
  plus extra for dusting
280 g/10 oz wholemeal flour
1^1/$_2$ tsp bicarbonate of soda
1 tsp salt
1 tsp dark muscovado sugar
about 425 ml/15 fl oz buttermilk

Chilli Cheese Cornbread

Preheat the oven to 200°C/400°F/Gas Mark 6. Grease a heavy 23-cm/9-inch cake tin or ovenproof frying pan and line the base with greaseproof paper. Sift the flour, baking powder and salt into a bowl, then stir in the polenta and 115 g/4 oz of the grated Cheddar cheese.

Pour the melted butter into a bowl and stir in the eggs and milk. Pour on to the dry ingredients, add the chilli, then mix quickly until just combined. Do not overmix.

Spoon the mixture into the prepared tin, scatter the remaining cheese on top and bake in the preheated oven for about 20 minutes, or until risen and golden. Leave to cool in the tin for 2 minutes, then turn out onto a wire rack to cool completely.

MAKES 1 LOAF

115 g/4 oz self-raising flour

1 tbsp baking powder

1 tsp salt

225 g/8 oz fine polenta

150 g/$5^1/_2$ oz grated mature Cheddar cheese

55 g/2 oz butter, melted, plus extra for greasing

2 eggs, beaten

300 ml/10 fl oz milk

1 fresh red chilli, deseeded and finely chopped

Herb Focaccia

Combine the flour, yeast, salt and sugar in a bowl and make a well in the centre. Gradually stir in most of the water and 2 tablespoons of the olive oil to make a dough. Gradually add the remaining water, if necessary, drawing in all the flour.

Turn out onto a lightly floured surface and knead. Transfer to a bowl and lightly knead in the herbs for 10 minutes, until soft but not sticky. Wash the bowl and lightly coat with olive oil.

Shape the dough into a ball, put it in the bowl and turn the dough over so it is coated. Cover tightly with a tea towel or lightly greased clingfilm and set aside in a warm place to rise until the dough has doubled in volume. Meanwhile, sprinkle polenta over a baking sheet.

Turn the dough out onto a lightly floured surface and knead lightly. Cover with the upturned bowl and leave for 10 minutes. Meanwhile, preheat the oven to 230°C/450°F/Gas Mark 8.

Roll out and pat the dough into a 25-cm/10-inch circle, about 1 cm/½ inch thick, and carefully transfer it to the prepared baking sheet. Cover the dough with a tea towel and leave to rise again for 15 minutes.

Using a lightly oiled finger, poke indentations all over the surface of the loaf. Drizzle over the remaining olive oil and sprinkle lightly with sea salt. Bake in the preheated oven for 15 minutes, or until golden and the loaf sounds hollow when tapped on the bottom. Transfer the loaf to a wire rack to cool completely.

MAKES 1 LOAF

400 g/14 oz strong white flour, plus extra for dusting

7 g/¼ oz easy-blend dried yeast

1½ tsp salt

½ tsp sugar

300 ml/10 fl oz warm water

3 tbsp extra virgin olive oil, plus extra for greasing

4 tbsp finely chopped fresh mixed herbs

polenta or cornmeal, for sprinkling

sea salt, for sprinkling

Olive Rolls

Stone the olives with an olive or cherry pitter and finely chop them. Pat off the excess brine or oil with kitchen paper. Set aside.

Combine the flour, salt and yeast in a bowl and make a well in the centre. Gradually stir in most of the water and the olive oil to make a dough. Gradually add the remaining water, if necessary, drawing in all the flour.

Lightly knead in the chopped olives and herbs. Turn out the dough onto a lightly floured surface and knead for 10 minutes, until smooth and elastic. Wash the bowl and lightly coat with oil.

Shape the dough into a ball, put it in the bowl and turn over so it is coated. Cover tightly with a tea towel or lightly oiled clingfilm and set aside to rise until it has doubled in volume. Meanwhile, preheat the oven to 220°C/425°F/Gas Mark 7 and dust a baking sheet with flour.

Turn out the dough onto a lightly floured surface and knead lightly. Roll the dough into 20-cm/8-inch ropes.

Cut the dough into 16 even pieces. Shape each piece into a ball and place on the prepared baking sheet. Cover and set aside to rise for 15 minutes.

Lightly brush the top of each roll with olive oil. Bake in the preheated oven for about 25–30 minutes, or until the rolls are golden brown. Transfer to a wire rack and set aside to cool completely.

MAKES 16 ROLLS

115 g/4 oz black or green olives in brine or oil, drained

750 g/1 lb 10 oz strong white flour, plus extra for dusting

$1^1/_2$ tsp salt

7 g/$^1/_4$ oz easy-blend dried yeast

450 ml/16 fl oz warm water

2 tbsp extra virgin olive oil, plus extra for brushing

4 tbsp finely chopped fresh oregano, parsley or thyme leaves, or 1 tbsp dried mixed herbs